MW01633737

Authored by Terry Carolyn Mudryk
'Ole' Fashioned Station Wellness Centre
5100 - 3rd Street, Box 369,
Boyle Alberta, Canada T0A 0M0
1-780-689-6736
www.oilersforlife.ca

Graphic Design & Page Layout by Next Phase Multimedia
www.nextphasemultimedia.com

Edited and Published by Kelly Falardeau - Mixx & Koki Publishing
BookKellyToSpeak@gmail.com

Photographs from Terry Mudryk family collection

ISBN # 978-1-989849-02-6

Copyright © 2018-2020 Terry Carolyn Mudryk. All rights reserved.
No part of this book, design, outline, illustrations, graphics
or personal family information may be reproduced or transmitted
in any form or by any means, including informational storage
and retrieval systems, without permission in writing from the publisher,
except for brief quotations that provide credit to
'I Can-cer Vive! Our Journey' by Terry Carolyn Mudryk

"Functional Science is the poorest and most impoverished topic."
~ Terry Carolyn Mudryk

Dedication

I dedicate this book to
Marty and Bryan -
when cancer strikes a sibling,
it becomes a family battle.

These two have come through so much adversity together with incredible support not just for each other, but always thinking of others who have been diagnosed and are following a similar path.

Both boys have raised a significant amount of money to help cancer patients and continue to do so through the BRYAN MUDRYK GOLF CLASSIC and the WILLIAMS AND MUDRYK 100 KM.

September 2017, Marty became President of Knight's Cabin, an organization that provides healing retreats to cancer survivors. Each retreat offers practical research-based counselling and awareness sessions with the end goal of increasing physical activity, improving nutrition, supporting sleep management, and assisting attendees with tools to effectively deal with stress and promote recovery.

Monies raised by the Classic will go to Knight's Cabin and their efforts. For more information visit www.knightscabin.com . I thank you for your support.

I could not be prouder of both my boys for their courage, their relentless determination to overcome life's challenges even when they become life-threatening, their ability to grasp the good days, put the tough days behind them, and conquer a new day. I am forever grateful for our strong family ties and the love we shared.

That love has been a powerful tool for both Bryan and I as we process grief, in the loss of a brother and a son. Each of us in our own journeys as we ride out the emotions of sadness and joy with memories we both have of Marty... because now a piece of our heart lives in Heaven.

From mom's heart to yours -
love you forever.

muddytsn

muddytsn Well I didn't throw up and they didn't fire me. Very honoured to call my first ever NHL game on a Saturday night in our nations capital. Ottawa versus Montreal is something I'll never forget! This one is dedicated to my family and mostly my brother Marty!

Table of Contents

Introduction: Our Journey... I Can-cer Vive   1

Chapter 1:   Leaky Gut   3

Chapter 2:   Avoid These Ten Food & Food Additives   7

Chapter 3:   Eight Ways to Living Chemical-Free   16

Chapter 4:   What Are Essential Oils?   27

Chapter 5:   Carrier Skin Oils That Will Work For You   31

Chapter 6:   Essential Oils and Cancer Research   36

Chapter 7:   The Science Behind Aromatherapy   38

Chapter 8:   Essential Oil Benefits for Cancer and Immunity   42

Chapter 9:   Thirteen More Support Therapies for Cancer and Disease   50

Chapter 10:   Herbs & Essential Oils - Simple Solutions, Healthy Choices   67

Chapter 11:   Terry's Timeless Recipes - Blended in "God's Pharmacy"   73

Chapter 12:   Healing with Crystals   92

Chapter 13:   Body, Mind & Soul - Feed the Soul   99

Chapter 14:   Gratitude - 365 Days of Gratefulness   103

Chapter 15:   Grief - Facing the Unexpected   106

Chapter 16:   Bryan's Story   111

Chapter 17:   Marty's Journey   121

Chapter 18:   From My Heart To Yours   139

Concluding Remarks   143

Advertisements   144

Resources   146

Reflections   147

Blank Pages for Notes   148

You are the one who holds the roadmap to your recovery and well-being. Research the many routes available to get you to your destination.

Introduction:

This book is about our healing journey - physical, emotional and spiritual - paving the way for research, but unknown territory. These are our personal findings in our battle with chronic disease. All information in this book is for educational purposes only and is not intended to substitute advice given by an oncologist, doctor, pharmacist or licensed health care professional.

This book is compiled with the understanding that the publisher or the author is not responsible nor liable for any misconceptions or misuse of information provided and shall have neither liability nor responsibility to any person or entity concerning any loss, damage, or injury caused directly or indirectly by the information contained in this book.

Our Journey... I Can-cer Vive

Our story is about radical lifestyle changes because we had no options. I have come to realize we take better care of our cars than we do of ourselves because we take our bodies for granted until something goes very wrong. We all need to make lifestyle changes.

Getting a call that your children have cancer is beyond any mother's worst nightmare. Words cannot describe the anguish, the anger, the fear of loss, and how incredibly heart-wrenching it is to watch the battle for survival. If this book can help just one person live better, then our purpose is not in vain.

Our story is somewhat unique. With the support of family and friends, we raised **$1.8 million** over fifteen years, all donated to the Cross Cancer Institute in Edmonton for medical equipment needed for research and testing patient diagnosis, and treatments. These vital pieces included such equipment as: a positron emission tomography (PET) imaging centre, electron microscope, the MR-Linac system, the Bruker preclinical Optical-X-ray imaging system, plus many others that enhance care and give patients specialized treatment options. More importantly this equipment can be used to examine other metastatic cancers such as breast and melanoma. Not only has it improved the lives of patients at the Cross Cancer Institute, but it has given the hospital a leading edge in advanced equipment and treatment plans.

Chemotherapy is not always an option, so we needed to find a working protocol through functional science medicine, which combines essentia oils, supplements, diet, alternative therapies and eliminating chemicals out of our lives.

I am a licensed Cosmetologist by trade, and I have my Advanced Reiki, Access Bars & Raindrop Therapies Certification. I am working on my 3rd and 4th level Aromatherapy and love working with essential oils. I teach Essential Oils 101 and Chemical Free Living classes - I am going to touch on twelve basic healthier living options that can help prevention of chronic disease or perhaps be life-saving.

Functional health science plays a huge part in our battle. We work alongside Corey Deacon of Neurvana Health with offices in Calgary and Red Deer, Alberta. He has his masters in neuroscience and natural health. Corey is an absolute blessing on testing and finding the root of the cause. Every known disease is directly or indirectly associated with the gut. Eliminating leaky gut and body infections are the critical factors to optimum health.

Here is what Corey Deacon, MSc, DNM, RTN, BCN. BCAMP, BCHHP, says about functional health science:

"Functional Medicine/Science evaluations allow us to uncover the cause(s) of someone's issues. These issues could be a diagnosed disease or condition such as depression or cancer. However, it can also be symptoms that aren't diagnosed with a disease/disorder such as brain fog, memory issues, or stress.

Functional science also looks at treating the person directly, rather than trying to treat symptoms or disease directly. This then brings into account a person's unique experience, development and genetics. For this reason, every person is treated differently depending on these factors.

Often there are multiple factors affecting someone's health. Until these factors are all addressed, people will not improve and not reach their health goals. For this reason, functional science requires in-depth testing of nervous system activity, blood, urine, stool, and saliva to determine underlying biochemistry in near totality.

Once these factors are uncovered, integrative strategies are used to reverse the issues and heal the client. These may include diet, lifestyle, nutritional supplementation, antimicrobials, detoxification, trauma therapy, neurofeedback, biological dentistry, upper cervical chiropractic, body work, and more. These strategies are integrated with precision and are unique to each."

You can find Corey's contact information in the Resources Page.

In this book, we will touch on factors that can potentially help you keep your immune system optimum for diffusing chronic disease. Many of our family members have improved their immune systems and have made progress with their chronic diseases including cancer.

Chapter 1

Leaky Gut

When we think about how rich our diets are, with processed foods that are high in sugars, it's no wonder that over half of our population suffers from some inflammation or chronic disease. While cancer is the worst, processed foods, chemicals, toxins and moulds, can also lead to heart disease, diabetes, chronic inflammation and so much more. Eliminating these free radicals out of your daily life can drastically reduce the risk of cancer and dramatically affect your survival, and is critical to your well-being.

Some of this can become overwhelming, but I encourage you to take small steps, make a change every week, and over time small changes become significant changes.

Leaky gut syndrome is not something taught in medical school, but instead points to a group of common symptoms that lead to the medical diagnosis.

More and more studies are finding that gut issues are the root cause of many autoimmune and chronic disease.

Leaky gut is caused by poor diet choices, toxic overload, bacterial imbalance, pharmaceuticals and chemicals that permeate our everyday lives.

Exposure to environmental chemicals is linked to various health disorders including obesity, type 2 diabetes, cancer, and dysregulation of the immune and reproductive systems.

With the surface area of about the size of a tennis court, our digestive tract accounts for 70% of our immune system and is a vital immune barrier protecting us from disease contamination.

Every day our gut relies on carefully maintaining microorganisms [the good guys], pathogens [the bad guys], and neutral bystanders. Experts believe the healthy mix of these microbes are about 85% good guys and 15% foes.

Toxins, nutrient deficient diet, stress, and medications, can cause the bad guys to take hold, burrow into the mucus of the gut wall and create holes in the intestinal lining that can change the pH balance of the gut and lead to yeast overgrowth.

When the gut wall is weakened [gut barrier] it no longer can control undigested food particles, microbes and toxins from leaking directly into the bloodstream, affecting the liver, pancreas, gallbladder, bile ducts, adrenals and the entire body. When leaky gut becomes chronic, the toxic potential of those roaming microbes means the leaky gut is no longer localized but becomes systematic that can have deadly health ramifications.

- **Candida gut** is directly related to yeast overgrowth and being overweight, is often caused by birth control pill and diet high in sugars.

- **Stressed gut** weakens your adrenals, kidneys, thyroid and can cause hormonal imbalance.

- **Immune gut** affects about fifteen million people who suffer from food allergies and fifty million adults with autoimmune disorders. It is usually triggered by taking prescription antibiotics and medications, and triggered by emotions of grief, depression and anger.

- **Gastric gut** is caused by small intestinal bacterial overgrowth and acid reflux caused by poor digestion and antacids, which often results in bloating, acid reflux or gas.

- **Toxic gut** can result in gallbladder disease, skin conditions and chronic liver issues. It develops when a diet high in bad fats and toxins overworks the gallbladder and liver. An estimated twenty million Americans have gallbladder disease. Getting more sleep is important for those with toxic gut because the body and especially the liver cleanse itself while you sleep from 1:00 a.m. to 3:00 a.m.

Recently, health studies have focused on the safety of glyphosate, and the mixture of ingredients in Roundup. Scientists found that Roundup's inert ingredients amplified the toxic effect on human cells and found they can kill human cells, particularly embryonic, placental and umbilical cells. About 100 million pounds of glyphosate is applied to American farms and yards and children's playgrounds every year. The EPA clarify glyphosate as a Group E chemical, which means there is substantial evidence that it does cause cancer in humans. Some studies have linked Roundup to non-Hodgkin's lymphoma. The French team led by Gilles-Éric Séralini, a University of Caen molecular biologist said its results highlight the need for health agencies to reconsider the safety of Roundup. As always, do your research on all chemicals you use in your personal space.

Antibiotics are the most profound disrupters of the gut microbiome. They cause antibiotic resistance, reduce vitamin absorption and damage the digestive lining causing leaky gut. Because of antibiotic overuse, certain bacteria have become resistant to even the most potent antibiotics available today.

The father of modern medicine Hippocrates said, "All disease begins in the gut."

Hundreds of years after his death, scientific research has now proven that he was right all those years ago. Thousands of research articles have been published since, demonstrating how modern diets and lifestyles have negatively impacted our gut flora.

Leaky gut merely is intestinal tight junction malfunction. Tight junctions have an exact job to maintain the delicate balance between allowing vital nutrients to enter your bloodstream while remaining small enough to prevent disease-causing compounds from passing out of your digestive tract into the rest of your body.

Leaky gut causes a host of serious illnesses and chronic diseases including cancer

Our family's battle with cancer and other inflammatory issues were a direct cause of leaky gut. There is always an underlying problem that causes cancer including mould, infections in the body and toxicants. They can also cause other chronic diseases.

For example, Candida is a fungus that aids in nutrient absorption and digestion when in proper levels in the body. When stress or other inhibitors cause it to overproduce, and it is left unchecked, it breaks down the walls of the intestinal lining and penetrates into the bloodstream. This releases by-product toxins and other toxins from your body causing chronic health conditions such as exhaustion, cravings for sweets, brain fog, joint pain, chronic allergies, and digestive problems. Most problematic is a very weakened immune system.

An overgrowth of the *Citrobacter freundii* bacteria is known to cause liver, gallbladder, bile duct, and pancreatic cancers. Recently it's been linked to cancer by two mechanisms: an introduction of chronic inflammation, and production of carcinogenic bacterial metabolites. The most specific example of an inflammatory mechanism of carcinogenesis is *Helicobacter pylori (H. pylori)* which have been linked to adenocarcinoma of the distal stomach by its propensity to cause lifelong inflammation. This inflammation is thought to cause cancer by inducing cell proliferation and production of mutagenic free radicals and N-nitroso compounds. H. pylori are the first bacterium to be termed a definite cause of cancer in humans by the International Agency for Research on Cancer. Mutagenic bacterial metabolites are also suspected to increase the risk for cancer best exemplified in colon cancer. More research is needed on the identification of bacterial causes of malignancy that could have significant implications for cancer prevention.

To heal leaky gut, you must address toxicity of your mind, body and emotions, work through forgiveness and self-righteousness.

Practice meditation, exercise to calm you and treat yourself to full body massages or therapies.

Eat organic and grass fed, avoid grains, avoid sugar, and remember to take your supplements; use essential oils, humanities oldest remedies, which remain the most effective.

All essential oils have hundreds of compounds and healing properties, with multiple benefits for your gut.

The good news is that many functional and integrative medicine practitioners have a greater understanding of this condition than they did five years ago. Testing is available to help you determine what underlying issues are the cause of your health deterioration.

For a detailed understanding of leaky gut, purchase the book "Eat Dirt" by Dr. Josh Axe in any Chapters Bookstore or online.

Signs and Symptoms of Leaky Gut

- *Digestive issues, gas, bloating, diarrhea, weight loss, fat malabsorption*
- *Seasonal allergies, asthma*
- *Hormonal imbalances, PMS, PCOS*
- *Diagnosis of an autoimmune disease*
- *Diagnosis of Chronic Fatigue Syndrome or Fibromyalgia*
- *Mood imbalances, anxiety, depression, ADD, ADHD*
- *Skin issues, acne, rosacea, eczema*
- *Gut infections, SIBO, Candida overgrowth, parasites*
- *Excess weight, obesity, diabetes*
- *Nutrient deficiency, anemia*
- *Brain fog*
- *Osteoporosis, osteopenia*
- *Frequent colds*
- *Joint pain, muscle pain*

Tissues of the Body Affected by Autoimmune Attack

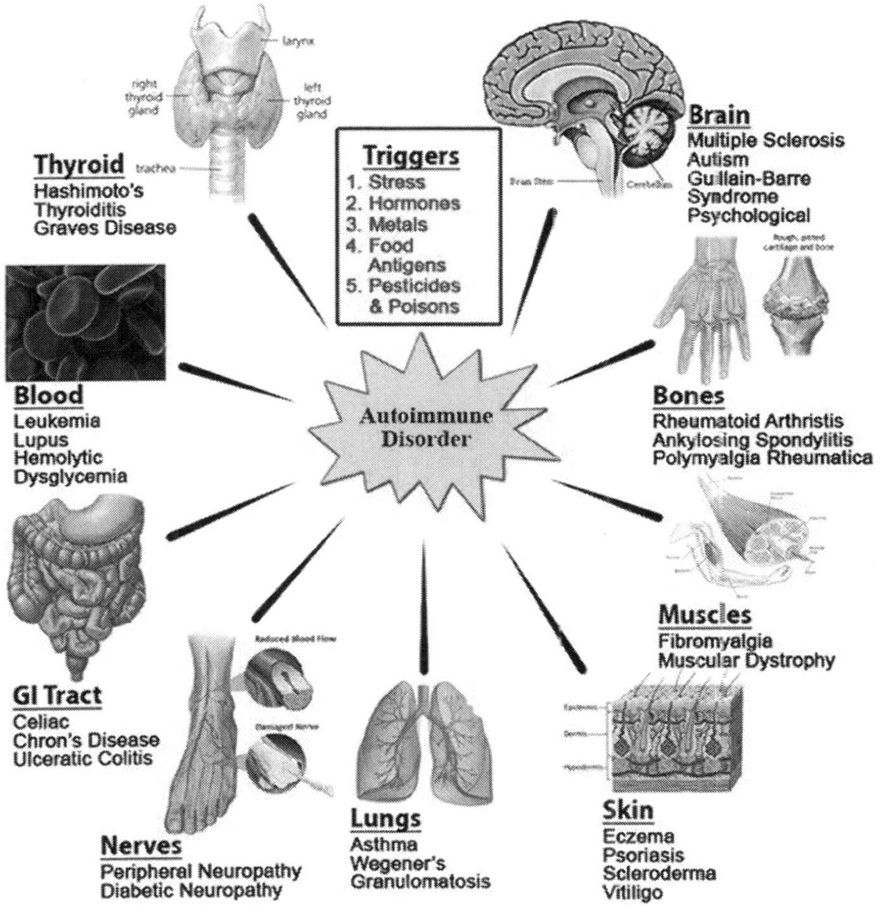

Many types of Cancers such as:
organ, musculoskeletal, glands, blood, breast, eye, lymph, ovarian & prostate

Chapter 2

Avoid These Ten Food & Food Additives

1 **GRAINS (white flour)** Herbicides and pesticides are laden heavily on our crops making it difficult to escape harm's way. All nutritional value is removed from refined white flour. The chemicals used in the bleaching process, such as chlorine gas, absorb into our bodies causing all sorts of gut issues. Carbohydrates are converted to sugar by our body; so excessive products that contain white flour can lead to insulin resistance the preferred fuel source for cancer.

Buy organic GMO-free flour, bread and flour products; always check the sugar content of products.

2 **GENETICALLY MODIFIED FOODS (GMO)** More than 90% of our corn and soy are now genetically modified and are added to thousands of products. This reasonably new practice has not had enough studies done to know the long-term effects on human health.

Look for GMO-free labels.

3 **SUGARS** High refined sugar intake has a strong correlation to tumour development in cancer patients. Research shows sugar can cause cancer. In 2013-14 the Journal of Clinic Investigation released the results of an in vitro study that analyzed the effects of increased sugar uptake and oncogenesis (cancer creation). The results demonstrated positive and direct evidence to early phases of cancer cell production.

Cancer cells uptake sugar at 10-12 times the rate of healthy cells. One of the crucial mechanisms through which cancer is promoted through sugar, is through mitochondrial dysfunction, because sugar burns very differently than fats, generating free radicals. When free radicals damage the mitochondria of the cell, the nuclear DNA, and cell membrane are also affected, leading to protein impairment.

Obesity and chronic overeating have had a positive correlation and causation to the growth and development of cancer cells. According to the Canadian Cancer Society, being obese can cause changes in hormone levels, increase insulin levels which in turn, increase the risk of developing breast, colon or uterine cancers.

Sugar has been related to a multitude of health problems, including diabetes, heart disease, stroke, immobility, elevated triglycerides and high blood pressure. Cutting out refined sugars from soda and processed foods is an excellent way to start decreasing your risk of cancer cell growth.

Hidden sugars include fructose, lactose, sucrose, maltose, glucose, dextrose, invert sugar, fruit juice, malt syrup, corn syrup, cane sugar and are all forms of nutritionally empty calories, and not all are necessarily listed on the ingredient list.

Use organic honey (free of pesticides & herbicides), agave or pure Canadian syrup in moderation; check labels for sugar content.

10 PLACES
SUGAR HIDES

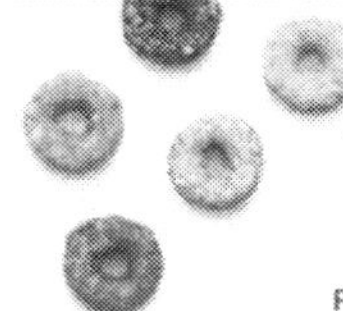

1 Cereals, including hot cereals like flavored oatmeal

2 Packaged breads, including "whole grain" kinds

3 Snack or granola bars

4 "Lower calorie" drinks, including coffees, energy drinks, blended juices and teas

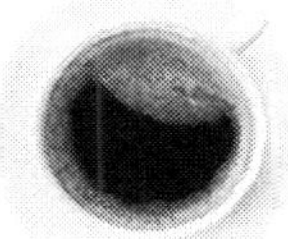

5 Protein bars and meal replacements

6 Sweetened yogurts and other dairy products (like flavored kefir, frozen yogurt, etc.)

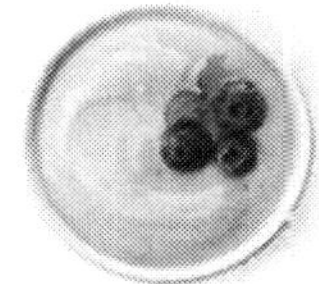

7 Frozen waffles or pancakes

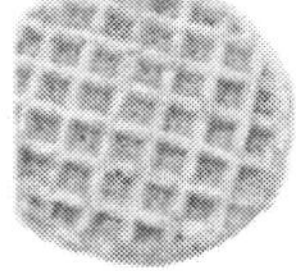

8 Bottled sauces, dressings, condiments and marinades (like tomato sauce, ketchup, relish or teriyaki, for example)

9 Dried fruit and other fruit snacks

10 Restaurant foods, where sugar is used in sauces, various desserts and dressings for extra flavor

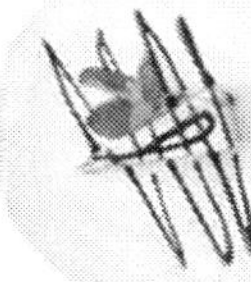

4 MICROWAVE POPCORN This product is the centre of lung cancer debates around the world: the dangers of the microwave itself, to the actual contents of GMO corn and oil (which the manufacturer does not have to disclose) unless its organic. The chemically lined bag and the fumes released from the artificial butter flavouring contain diacetyl, which both are toxic to humans.

Make your own popcorn the old fashioned way with GMO-free kernels.

How Safe Are Microwaves?

When my youngest son was diagnosed with cancer, I researched the pros and cons of using a microwave and had no doubt in my mind I could live life without one. That was in 1996, and I have had a toaster oven in its place ever since.

Do I believe microwaves are safe? With my son in a 3-year battle, why would I risk exposing him to electromagnetic fields (EMF) generated by magnetrons that vibrate at a speed of 2.4 billion times per second? That's what causes water molecules in the food to resonate at very high frequencies and generate heat.

Microwaves need to meet standards set by the FDA. Those standards limit the amount of microwave radiation to five milliwatts (mW) of its lifetime which is approximately two inches from the oven surface. Even new microwaves emit significant levels of microwave energy so what that means is, these EMF's permeate into your home.

In May of 2011, the World Health Organization classified this type of EMF exposure as a Group 2B carcinogen. Added to this, microwave ovens, cables, and motors also give off high magnetic fields, often over ten milligauss. Exposures of just four milligauss of a magnetic field, have been firmly linked to leukemia and thus categorized as carcinogenic.

Microwaving meats to ensure sanitary ingestion promotes the formation of a well-known carcinogen called d-Nitrosodienthanolamines.

Swiss clinical trials have found microwaving food increases cholesterol levels. It was also found to decrease red and white blood cell counts while reducing hemoglobin and producing radiolytic compounds.

Russian and Japanese studies have shown how food loses nearly 60% to 90% of its food value when cooked or heated in a microwave. Food can also lose up to 97% of its beneficial antioxidants.

Cooking with plastics, paper containers, and packaged containers can leak carcinogenic toxins into your diet such as polyethylene terephthalate (PET).

Benzene, toluene, and xylene can leach out of packages of common foods such as pizzas, popcorn, and fast foods.

The University of Minnesota published the following in 1989: "Although microwaves heat food quickly, they are not recommended for heating baby's formula because heating the bottle in a microwave can cause changes in the milk and a loss of vitamins. In expressed breast milk some of the protective properties may be destroyed. Warm the baby's milk in a warm bowl of water; it may take longer but is safer."

Dr. Hans Ulrich Hertel, who worked as a food scientist for many years, was the first scientist to conceive and carry out a quality clinical study on the effects microwaved nutrients have on the blood and physiology of the human body. He worked alongside Dr. Bernard H. Blanc of the Swiss Federal Institute of Technology in the University Institute for Biochemistry. The summary of their results is shocking that microwaves are still sold today to the unsuspecting and trusting consumers.

I love the safety of my toaster oven; it only takes a few seconds longer to melt butter or warm up leftovers. I pop corn the old fashioned way on the stove, and use non-GMO popping corn.

It is not worth the risk of my family's health, nor the loss of essential food nutrients. Check out https://www.cancer.org or www.health-science.com for more information on the dangers of microwaves.

5 CANNED GOODS   Most cans are lined with bispherol-A (BPA) which is known to alter the brain cells of rats genetically. Many plastic goods and food containers use BPA.

Buy organic fresh or frozen and cook from scratch; buy BPA-free containers. Always research your sources.

6 FARMED FISH   Avoid at all costs. Farmed fish are crammed in small crowded environments, treated with antibiotics, pesticides, and other carcinogenic chemicals to try to control the bacterial, viral & parasitic outbreaks! Farmed salmon also have less omega-3 than wild salmon.

Buy wild salmon.

7 HYDROGENATED OILS   While extracted from their source, oils are chemically treated to change the smell, colour and taste. Ever wonder why you see three or four shades of canola oil on the grocery shelf or olive oil in different shades of green? Chemicals! Chemicals! Chemicals! Notwithstanding, also be sure the source is chemical free.

Always buy organic, first cold press & unrefined. (your oils will be darker, have a more pungent aroma and perhaps have residue in the bottle which just means it's healthier for you).

8 CARBONATED DRINKS   Filled with high-fructose, corn syrup, dyes and a host of other chemicals, they provide ZERO nutritional value to your body. The word "diet" only means it contains aspartame, sucralose, saccharin or some other artificial sweeteners that are linked to a cascade of harmful metabolic and neurological effects. While health agencies claim they are safe, the science says otherwise.

Drink more water, organic green and herb teas.

9 SALTED, PICKLED & SMOKED FOODS   These products contain preservatives such as nitrates which prolong shelf life. Over time they collect in your body and cause damage at the cellular level that leads to chronic diseases like cancer. When cooked at high temperatures, the nitrates convert to more dangerous nitrates.

Note that these do not include home preserves. Buy homemade preserves at farmers markets or small home-based businesses.

10 FOODS THAT CONTAIN ASPARTAME, MSG, ARTIFICIAL COLOURS & PRESERVATIVES
Aspartame and glutamate act as neurotransmitters in the brain by facilitating the transmission of information from neuron to neuron. Too much aspartate or glutamate in the brain kills certain neurons by allowing the influx of too much calcium into the cells. This

flow triggers excessive amounts of free radicals, which destroy the cells, referred to as excitotoxins they excite or stimulate the neural cells to death.

Expert, Professor Olney, a neuroscientist and researcher in the Department of Psychiatry, School of Medicine, Washington University, and one of the world's foremost authorities on excitotoxins, informed Searle in 1971, that aspartic acid caused holes in the brains of mice. For more information, read a very interesting book "Excitotoxins: The Taste That Kills" by Russell L. Blaylock, MD.

A few of the many chronic illnesses shown to be contributed by long-term exposure to aspartame & glutamate are: headaches, dizziness, seizures, nausea, depression, muscle spasms, vision problems, weight gain, and joint pain. These lead to chronic diseases such as fibromyalgia, epilepsy, MS, chronic fatigue, lymphoma, and Parkinson's disease.

Aspartame is made up of three chemicals: aspartic acid, phenylalanine, and methanol. The book "Prescription for Nutritional Healing" by James and Phyllis Balch, lists aspartame under the category of "chemical poison."

KETOSIS, KETONES - This Could Be Your Ticket To Wellness

Many of you have heard about a KETOSIS diet. I would have to say it's a lifestyle change versus a diet. Nutritional ketosis, in which the body burns fat rather than sugar for fuel, is a powerful approach to radically improving health that's achieved by eating a high, good fat, low carb, moderate protein diet.

This lifestyle change does not focus on calories but allows you the freedom and flexibility to eat what is right for you.

Whether you are struggling with weight problems, autoimmune conditions, chronic health like cancer or just feel sluggish and depressed; this could be your ticket to wellness.

Most people are rarely in ketosis and never experience its benefits because the body prefers sugars as its primary fuel source, especially over the last fifty years when everything we purchase that is processed is infiltrated with sugar. Our bodies use up much of the nutrients we eat every day and that is quite a lot of calories, however, if we overeat or overeat sugar enriched foods, then the body puts it in storage that we call excess fat.

The body breaks down fat into fatty acids and glycerol, which can be used for fuel in the cells directly, but not for the needs of your brain. To meet your brain's needs, the fatty acids and the glycerol enter the liver where they are converted into sugar and ketones. The glycerol undergoes a process called gluconeogenesis which converts to sugar, while fatty acids are converted into ketones (ketogenesis).

As a result of ketogenesis, a ketone body called acetoacetate is produced which is converted into two types of ketone bodies:

1. Beta-hydroxybutyrate (BHB) - In general studies, it shows that the body and brain prefer using BHB and acetoacetate for energy because the cells can use it 70% more efficiently than glucose.

2. Acetone - which can sometimes be metabolized into glucose, but mostly is expelled as waste, gives off the distinct, smelly breath that most people doing Ketosis know.

The ketosis diet is much safer and healthier than the ketosis you get from fasting; the process of ketosis is closely regulated by the liver, and the body rarely produces more ketones than it needs for fuel.

Benefits of ketosis stimulate new mitochondrial that are formed in cells that burn ketones for fuel. They are important because they improve energy production and health of the cells.

Ketones help preserve the function of aging nerve cells and aid in the regeneration of damaged and malfunctioning nervous system cells. Studies have found that ketones help acute brain injuries improve significantly.

Ketones act as an antioxidant because they are a more efficient source of fuel than sugar. Ketones produce less reactive oxygen species and free radicals than sugar when they are used, thus allowing the body to protect itself from the damage that these free radicals and reactive oxygen species can cause.

Especially important and a critical part of our cancer battle is that research shows that ketones can fight various types of cancers including liver, lung and adrenal. We have seen shrinkage in both liver and lung cancer, using the keto lifestyle, plus functional science protocol mentioned in this book. It is working for our family not just to rid cancer cells but overall better body health.

Most cancer cells cannot use ketones as fuel; without fuel, the cancer cells have no energy for growth, and the immune system can finally eliminate them from the body.

Ketones improve the brain function immensely, especially people with autism, epilepsy, Alzheimers, and Parkinson's disease. Scientists are just beginning to understand the effects ketones have on the body and the positive results it shows on many chronic disease issues.

There are no downsides to Keto unless insulin is unavailable or not functioning properly, at which point ketoacidosis may occur. *[Source: https:ruled.me/benefits-ketogenic-diet/]*

You can find many Keto recipe books in bookstores and online. Always consult with your health practitioner to be sure you make the best choices for optimum health.

Keto... What You Can Eat

Meats...
Beef (includes hamburger & steak) / lamb / veal
Pork, including bacon, ham, processed sausages, pepperoni, hot dogs (can cause
inflammation and complicate the healing process for cancer patients or chronically ill)

Poultry...
Chicken / turkey / duck (buy organic, grass-fed when possible)

Eggs... no limit; eat as many as you wish

Fish and Shellfish...
Tuna / salmon / catfish / bass / trout / shrimp / scallops / crab / lobster
 (wild/ocean-fresh where possible; avoid farmed fish)

Salad Greens... max 2 cups/day
Lettuce (all varieties) / arugula / kale / spinach
Endive / radicchio / bok choi / chard / radishes / watercress
Greens - all varieties including beet, collards, mustard, and turnip
Chives / scallions (spring onion) / parsley
Cabbage - all varieties

Fibrous Vegetables... max 1 cup/day
Artichokes / asparagus / broccoli / brussel sprouts / bamboo shoots / bean sprouts /
 cauliflower / celery / celeriac (celery root) / chayote / cucumber / edamame
 beans / eggplant (aubergine) / green beans / jicama (in moderation) / mushrooms /
 okra / peppers / pumpkin / snow peas / sprouts (bean and alfalfa) / sugar snap peas /
 summer squash / tomatoes / turnip / zucchini (courgette)

Fatty Vegetables...
Black or green olives (up to 6/day)
Avocado (half a fruit/day)

Cheese... max 4 oz/day
Swiss / cheddar / brie / mozzarella / gruyere / goat / cream cheese

Cream... max 2 tbsp/day
Heavy / light / sour cream; not half & half; not condensed or evaporated milk (check
 ingredients and avoid those with modified corn starch &/or modified milk products)

Mayonnaise... max 2 tbsp/day (check sugar content)

Berries... limited (i.e. - 1/4 cup/day)
Blueberries / strawberries / raspberries / blackberries / huckleberries / gooseberries /
 salmon berries / goji berries

Condiments... (check sugar content)
Lemon / lime juice (up to 4 tsp/day) *or use 2-3 drops NHP essential oil
Yellow mustard (up tp 2 tbsp/day)
Soy sauce (up to 4 tbsp/day)
Salt and vinegar (no restrictions)
Ketchup / BBQ sauce (low carb & low sugar versions only)

Pickles...
Recipes with dill or garlic usually have no added
 sugar; avoid pickled foods with added sugars
 (homemade recipes are best)

Snacks...
Nuts / pumpkin seeds / sunflower seeds
Beef/turkey/chicken slices
Peanut butter (organic)
Deviled eggs
'Fat Bombs' / 'Keto Muffins'

For a printable list of 148 Low Carb Foods, visit:
https://ketosizeme.com/wp-content/uploads/2016/09/Printable-List-of-the-Carbs-In-Food.pdf

Throughout the widely researched topic of pork versus cancer, all agree that pork is high in inflammatory Omega-6 fats. In Canada, pigs consume mostly grains and seed oils which significantly increases the omega-6 fats in their systems. Pigs also consume just about anything alive, sick, or dead, making them a breeding ground for potentially dangerous infections. The meat and fat of a pig absorb toxins like a sponge. Their meat can be thirty times more toxic than beef or venison.

After eating beef or venison, the body takes up to eight or nine hours to digest so what toxins are eaten are processed slowly and can be excreted. Pork, on the other hand, takes four hours to digest and we get a much higher dosage of toxins in a much shorter timeframe. Unlike other mammals, a pig does not sweat or perspire, a body's means to remove toxins, so this too magnifies the issue of toxins. A pig has twice as much fat as beef. A T-bone steak contains 8.5 grams of fat, while a 3 oz. pork chop contains 18 grams of fat

Even prolonged cooking of pork cannot kill retroviruses and parasites that the meat harbours. Pigs carry about thirty diseases easily transferred to humans. They also have over a dozen parasites within them, such as tapeworms, flukes, and trichinae; there is no safe temperature for cooking pork enough to ensure these parasites and their eggs are killed.

One of the diseases found in pork is Porcine Reproductive and Respiratory Syndrome (PRRS) which attacks the swine's immune system, especially the lungs. Recent studies show PRRS can also be airborne. The Nepal Virus discovered in 1999, is said to cause the deadly encephalitis (acute brain inflammation). The third disease is Porcine Endogenous Retrovirus (PERV) found in the pig's genetics. A study conducted by Lancet says PERV can infect human cells and could spread to people who receive pig organs. The Menangle Virus discovered in 1976, causes pigs to give birth to deformed piglets. It can spread and affect humans as well.

Dr. Paul Jaminet, a trained astrophysicist who co-authored the book Perfect Health Diet, says that most American pork is processed and includes smoked ham, sausage, bacon, processed lunch meats, hot dogs, salami and other forms of processed pork. The problematic issue here is the nitrates added to the meats as a preservative, colouring and flavoring, are converted into nitrosamines, which are associated with an increased risk of certain cancers. Processed meats that are smoked during the curing process, also produce carcinogenic polycyclic aromatic hydrocarbons.

The World Health Organization reported, that according to studies done, for every 50 grams of processed meats someone eats per day (the equivalent of one hot dog), your risk of colorectal cancer goes up by 18%. In his report "The Adverse Influence of Pork Consumption on Health" Professor Hans-Heinrich Reckeweg says consumption of freshly killed pork products causes acute responses, such as inflammation of the appendix and gallbladder, biliary comics, acute catarrh, gastroenteritis with typhoid and paratyphoid symptoms, as well as severe eczema, carbuncles, sudoriparous abscesses, cancers, plus more.

The high content of omega-6 (linked to cirrhosis of the liver), the risk of infections to a stressed immune system, and adding potential harmful toxins found in processed pork meat, has health

practitioners advising against pork consumption especially for cancer patients.

Research studies such as Nanji and Norad (Norad spends approximately $600 million annually on the development of new knowledge) looked for diseases that correlate with pork consumption and hit upon multiple sclerosis, liver cirrhosis, and liver cancer.

If they were to rank popular meats by their healthfulness, in order from first to last, the list looks like this: beef, lamb, goat, duck, chicken, turkey, goose, and last pork.

On a side note, both of my son's functional science doctors recommended no pork due to the inflammation risk factor. One of his holistic doctors who practiced for over 35 years, saw healing occur faster when pork was eliminated from the diet.

What's unfortunate is that today we cannot rely on big food corporations to label their products accurately, and many hot dogs labelled 'pork free' still contain pork.

Buyer beware; buy from a known reputable local company who has grass fed, organic meats. You can find these at Planet Organic and your local Farmers' Market.

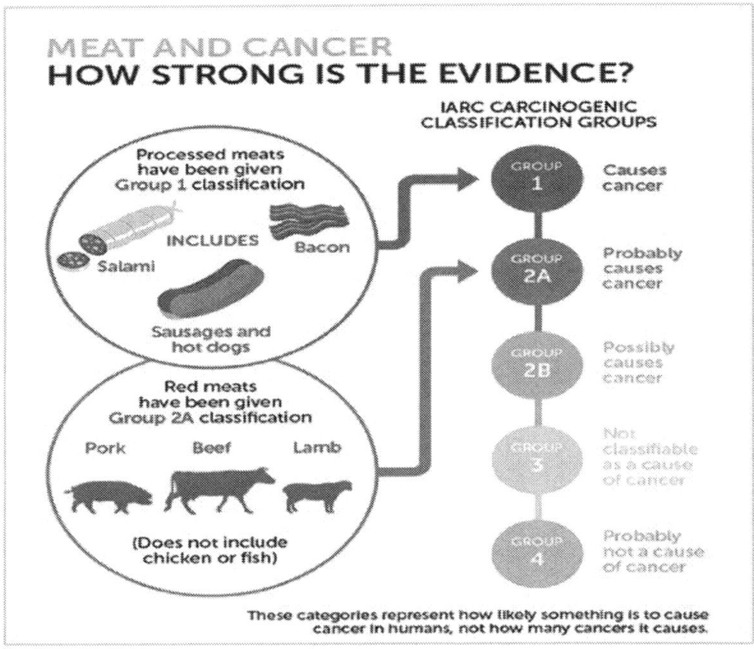

Reference: Nanji AA, Narod S Multiple sclerosis, latitude and dietary fat; the missing link? 1986
http://pmid.us/363877

Chapter 3

Eight Ways to Living Chemical-Free

When a diagnosis is made and a timeline is given, you have no options; you have twenty-four hours to turn it around. Mind boggling to say the least, and where do you start?

Chemicals are everywhere, and the government is quick to protect what they call company secrets. Dirty secrets! Did you know if your label on the shampoo, conditioner, hand cream, or shaving cream reads "fragrance" or "perfume," it is loaded with seventy to 200 chemicals that make them smell nice, with a good chance one being phthalates which are known endocrine disrupters? Men with higher phthalate compounds in their blood have reduced sperm counts according to studies done at the Harvard School of Public Health. The word "unscented" is made up of chemicals to trick your mind into thinking there is no fragrance. However, they contain chemicals, nevertheless.

Regarding household cleaners, there is no safety standard nor testing data or notification before bringing a product to market.

The average household contains about sixty-five toxic chemicals. More than eighty thousand human-made chemicals are put into our household products and food with a majority not tested for safety beforehand.

Ten thousand additives are allowed in food and food packaging. Food packaging often contains bisphenol - a [bpa] bisphenol-S [bps] and phthalates - that can migrate into your food. Propylparaben, used as a food preservative, is an endocrine-disruptor, making it relevant to estrogen-sensitive cancers like breast cancer. This chemical is found in about fifty brand name foods including tortillas, muffins, cakes and food dyes.

In Europe, propylparaben has been removed from its list of safe food additives, as well as more than 1,300 chemicals are banned from use in lotions, soaps, toothpaste and other personal care products. In the U.S. only eleven chemicals have been removed. Toxic flame retardants have been added to children's clothing - especially pyjamas, furniture like sofas and mattresses, baby products and electronics. Your mattress and bedding may be soaked in toxic flame retardants, but you will not find them listed on any of the labels.

Many of these chemicals end up in household dust, and young children could ingest 50 milligrams of household dust a day; making house dust an important source of toxic exposure. Many of these toxic flame-retardant chemicals have been linked to congenital disabilities, infertility, neurodevelopmental delays, reduced IQ and behavioural problems in children, hormonal disrupters, and cancer.

When we are exposed to them daily, weekly, and over a lifetime, in combinations, it is impossible to gauge the risks. Manufacturers argue that in small amounts these toxic chemicals are safe, but toxic chemicals can enter your body through the skin in twenty-eight seconds, in two minutes are in your bloodstream, and in twenty minutes go into every organ.

Fragrance and perfume (not to be mistaken for essential oil smells which are discussed in a later chapter) are the next second-hand smoke epidemic. They can cause instant headaches, rashes, difficulty in breathing and have been linked to cancer, asthma, reproductive disorders, hormone disruption and neurotoxicity.

Dryer sheets, car fresheners, air fresheners, scented candles, dish soap, hand soap, hand sanitizers, laundry soap, laundry fabric softener, scented toilet paper, deodorants, personal toiletries, baby powder, all petroleum-based products, lip balms & lipsticks, all have negative ramifications on your family's health.

We eat on average ten pounds of lip products a year, most chemical based. Spray room fresheners contain over eighty toxic chemicals including genotoxins, bronchoconstrictor, neurotoxins, reproductive toxins, hepatotoxins and mutagenic toxins. It's no wonder we know someone who is being diagnosed with cancer every week.

How to Become a Chemical/Toxic Free Household? Make Healthier Choices!

1. **BHA and BHT**: Endocrine disruptor, Carcinogen, Bioaccumulation;
 - *used mainly in cosmetics as preservatives*
2. **Coal Tar Dyes**: Carcinogen and heavy metal toxicity;
 - *processed foods, lipstick, hair dyes*
3. **DEA-Related Ingredients**: Carcinogen;
 - *creamy or foaming products such as moisturizers and shampoos*
4. **Dibutyl Phthalate**: Endocrine disruptor, reproductive toxicant;
 - *used in nail care products*
5. **Formaldehyde-Releasing Preservatives**: Carcinogen;
 - *used in a variety of cosmetics as preservatives*
6. **Parabens**: Endocrine disruptors, may interfere with male reproduction;
 - *used in a variety of cosmetics as preservatives*
7. **Parfum/Fragrance**: Carcinogen, Neurotoxocity, Allergies and sensitivities;
 - *used in a variety of cosmetics as preservatives*
8. **PEG Compounds**: Can be contaminated with 1.4-dioxine which may be a Carcinogen;
 - *cosmetic cream bases*
9. **Petrolatum**: Carcinogen;
 - *used in hair products for shine, moisture barrier in lipsticks/balms*
10. **Siloxanes**: Endocrine disruptor, reproductive toxicant;
 - *used in cosmetics to soften, smooth and moisten*
11. **Sodium Laureth Sulfate**: Carcinogen;
 - *used in foaming cosmetics, shampoos, cleaners, bubble baths*
12. **Triclosan**: Endocrine disruptor, Antibiotic resistance;
 - *toothpaste, cleansers, antiperspirants*

I recommend that everyone loads a free app called *Think Dirty* and research what you buy. This app tells you how carcinogenic the product is, how many hormonal disruptors, as well as allergens. For example, most store-bought toothpaste is '8' on the scale. That's chemicals that we brush our teeth with every single day. Be wise to the fact that even if it's low on the numbered scale, that does not mean it's okay, especially if it has fragrance on the label. Remember, manufacturers do not have to disclose those chemicals. Also, note that not everything in a health food store is healthy. You need to take that responsibility for you and your family and do your research.

1   **Buy from a reputable WELLNESS company** who you trust with your health.

Avoid aerosols, scented candles, and air fresheners.
Diffuse and use essential oils instead. Open windows for natural fresh air when possible.

Avoid dish soaps, hand soaps, and antibacterial products that contain TRICLOSAN.
Studies have found dangerous amounts of triclosan in rivers and streams where it is toxic to algae. Can you imagine how much goes into our environment, poisoning everything in its path? Rivers and streams are drinking sources for many of us.

Avoid QUATS (Quarternary Ammonium Compounds) found in fabric softeners, dryer sheets and most household cleaners. There is evidence that QUATS are the leading cause of asthma. Use wool balls with fifteen drops of your favourite essential oils. For added static control, crumple several grapefruit size balls of aluminum foil. I cannot stress enough, the importance of sleeping on toxic free sheets and wearing toxic-free clothing.

Avoid Butoxyethanol found in window cleaners, kitchen and multi-purpose cleaners. It gives these products a sweet smell but belongs in the category of glycol ethers. When inhaled, it causes sore throats and can contribute to narcosis, pulmonary edema, and severe liver and kidney damage. Clean your mirrors with newspaper and diluted water or make your own (I have many natural recipes easy to make and ready to share).

Green, natural, or biodegradable does not necessarily mean toxic free. Manufacturers use words to make it sound like you are buying smart when in fact it's just another marketing ploy. Research, research, research.

You can use many natural products to clean your home like baking soda, salt, vodka, essential oils, castile soap, and microfibre cloths.

Chemicals are in our clothes, furniture, pillows, blankets, sheets, baby and children's clothes, stuffies which all contain fire retardants, and poly chemicals, so please wash (with chemical-free detergent) your recently purchased clothing, pillows, sheets and everything new.

Buy wool and silk comforters, pillows, mattresses, and mattress pads. Bamboo pillows are not your best option. The shredded memory foam is encased with a cover that contains a bamboo-derived material called viscose rayon which requires the viscose process to be spun in carbon disulphide, a highly toxic chemical linked to cancer and numerous development effects. Hypoallergenic is just a label. According to WebMD, there aren't any standards for manufacturers on the use of "hypoallergenic" to describe a product which means they can label it without any testing.

Bamboo toothbrushes are not always what companies claim. I guess one way to test is the burn test. If the bristles melt, they are likely a polyester/ petroleum-based plastic or nylon.

Researching everything that you have thus far taken for granted to be safe for you and your family, is your best cancer and chronic disease prevention.

Many of these chemicals not only raise havoc with our health but interfere with brain development in children, act as immune suppressants and as in my son's case ultimately cause cancer. Very conclusive tests that we had taken were sent to the USA and indicated the cancer was caused by chemical compounds that the body was not able to detox. We take so much for granted that safety standards are set in place for the best interests of our health. It's very disappointing to find that is far from the truth. As moms and dads, it is our responsibility once we know better to do better for our families. I carry this message to every class I teach so that our story can be a happy ending for your family.

8 Most importantly, change your toiletries: shampoos, conditioners, hair sprays, makeup remover, makeup, hand soap, underarm deodorant, wear essential oils instead of perfume (much healthier choice), shaving cream, and aftershave. Most of us come in contact with more than 200 chemicals EVERY SINGLE DAY. Our liver, kidney and skin struggle to detox those toxins, eventually succumbing to these free radicals that can alter or damage our DNA and mutate our cell structure.

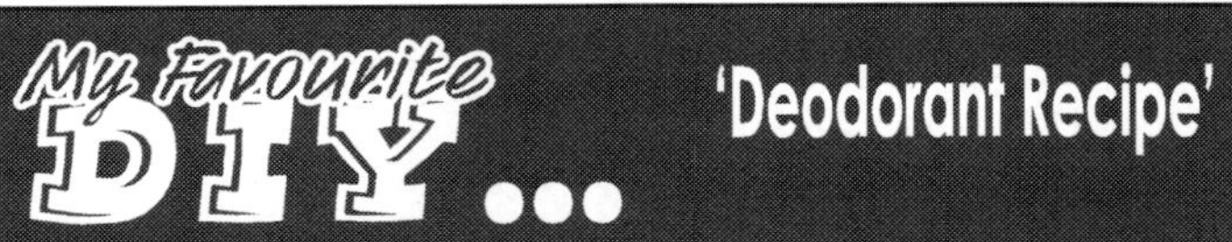

Combine in a pot and heat until just melted (do not overheat):
 4 tablespoons beeswax
 1/4 cup coconut oil
 3/4 cup unrefined organic shea butter
 1/4 teaspoon Vitamin E

Mix in:
 1 teaspoon baking soda
 1 cup arrowroot powder
- stir well

Add:
 20 drops FRANKINCENSE
 20 drops LAVENDER
 20 drops PEPPERMINT
 40 drops PURIFICATION
 25 drops SPRUCE
 20 drops CYPRESS
 20 drops BALSAM FIR

- stir and pour into a deodorant roll-on container. Cool until solid.

Our entire family uses this deodorant, and it works well, is chemical free and has absolutely no hormonal disruptors.

What is in Your Sunscreen?

Sunscreen blocks vitamin D production; vitamin D is an essential nutrient for health and cancer prevention. Lack of sunlight means lack of vitamin D, which is necessary for the body's immune system to function correctly. Low levels of vitamin D are linked to health problems including cancer. Appropriate sun exposure helps maintain adequate levels of vitamin D. Using sunscreen interferes with that exposure.

Most major brands of sunscreen block UVB (have a shorter wavelength and cause sunburns). UVB is required to produce vitamin D, so blocking it seems contradictory to good health and cancer prevention.

UVA has a longer wave, also known as tanning rays, and causes skin wrinkling and more damage to the skin, but both types of UV rays are attributable to skin cancer.

Sunscreen often contains cancer-causing chemicals that bake into the skin and get absorbed into the bloodstream within minutes of application, over-taxing the liver with toxins.

Check your sunscreen for these cancer-causing ingredients!

1. **OMC** - octal methoxycinnamate - in research has been shown to kill mouse cells even at low doses, but particularly toxic when exposed to the sun.

2. **TITANIUM DIOXIDE** - has been classified as a potential occupational carcinogen by the National Institute for Occupational Safety and Health.

3. **OXYBENZONE** - becomes carcinogenic when exposed to the sun and has been found to be a hormonal disruptor. The Environmental Working Group recommends consumers avoid this chemical, yet it remains in many sunscreens.

4. **RETINOL and RETINYL PALMITATE** - about half of the sunscreens tested contain derivatives of vitamin A such as retinol and retinyl palmitate, which by the FDA'S studies, found these ingredients to be photocarcinogenic, meaning the ingredients become toxic and cancer-causing when exposed to sunlight.

5. **DIISOPROPYL** - A study done in 2006 by the National Toxicology Program reported this ingredient increased the incidence of tumours in lab animals.

We keep hearing through mainstream media, to apply frequent and generous amounts of sunscreen to prevent skin cancer, when in fact if they contain the toxic ingredients mentioned, they can do far more harm than good.

Getting safe UV exposure alone does not cause skin cancer. The general recommendation is to get 15 to 30 minutes a day of direct sunlight to maintain adequate levels of vitamin D. Wear a hat and protective clothing to protect the skin from burning instead of using sunscreen. Always research the ingredients in your sunscreen. Use natural or non-toxic brands or make your own using natural ingredients such as coconut oil, shea butter, red raspberry seed oil and essential oils.

2 oz. RED RASPBERRY oil (close to the protection you would get from titanium dioxide in a natural form)
2 oz. organic avocado oil
1/2 teaspoon Vitamin E
1 tablespoon non-nano zinc oxide (will not absorb into the skin)
50 drops organic carrot seed essential oil
40 drops MYRRH
10 drops HELICHRYSUM
20 drops LAVENDER

Combine all the ingredients, making sure you use unadulterated essential oils. Apply every hour if exposed to the high sun, keep your sun exposure in check, and be "sun safe"!

Always research and make healthy choices for you and your family. Make these changes before you have no choice. Practice preventive measures. Our families went overnight chemical-free with all products from one wellness company. If you are interested in those products, please ask. My contact information is in the Resources Page.

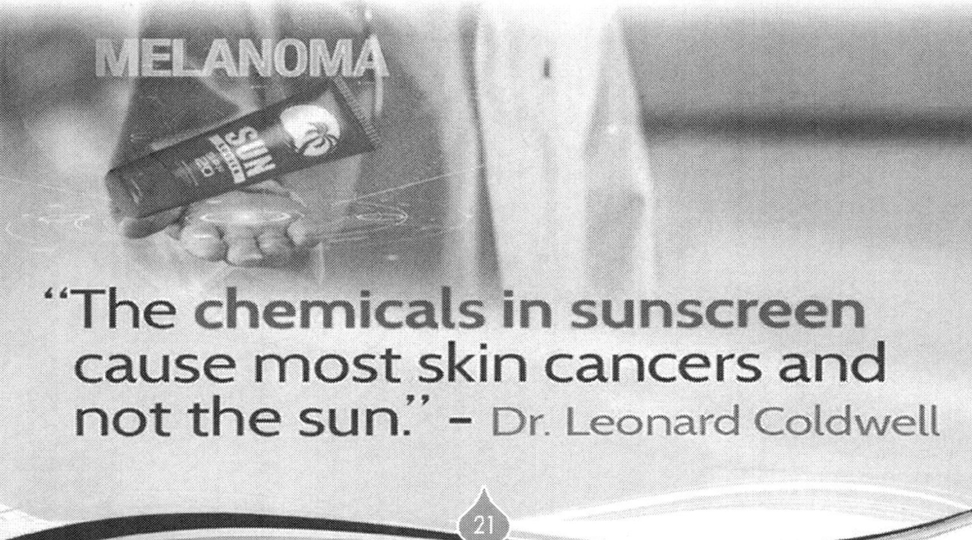

Smoking and Alcohol Addictions are at Higher Risk for Cancer

Lung cancer is the most common cancer worldwide, accounting for 1.2 million new cases annually: followed by cancer of the breast, over 1 million colorectal, 940,000 stomach, and 870,000 liver. Lung cancer strikes 900,000 men and 330,000 women yearly. Among men, smoking causes more than 80% of lung cancer cases. In women, smoking is the cause of 45% of all cancers worldwide, but more than 70% in North America. Unfortunately those numbers are rising rapidly.

Tobacco use is the major preventable cause of cancer in the world. Cigarette smoke contains over 4,000 chemicals including 70 known cancer causing (carcinogenic) compounds and 400 other toxins. These cigarette ingredients include nicotine, tar, and carbon monoxide, as well as formaldehyde, ammonia, hydrogen cyanide, arsenic, and DDT. Nicotine is highly addictive.

An electronic cigarette or e-cigarette is a device that tries to create the feeling of tobacco smoking and they too are filled with 3 to 4 times more nicotine than cigarettes. These products contain substances that increase the risk of oral and oropharyngeal cancer.

Secondhand smoke causes lung cancer in adults and children who have never smoked. Non smokers who are exposed to secondhand smoke at home or work increase their risk of developing lung cancer by 20-30% and causes over 7,300 lung cancer deaths among U.S. non-smokers each year.

Infants who are exposed to secondhand smoke are at greater risk for SIDS. Chemicals in secondhand smoke appear to affect the brain in ways that interfere with its regulation of infants breathing. Infants who die from SIDS have higher concentrations of nicotine in their lungs and higher levels of cotinine (a biological marker for secondhand smoke exposure) than infants who die from other causes. Studies show older children whose parents smoked get sick more often. Wheezing and coughing are more common in children who breathe secondhand smoke, and have more severe and frequent asthma attacks. They also get more ear infections and more operations to put ear tubes for drainage. Protect your children from the health hazards of secondhand smoke. *[U.S. Department of Health and Human Centres for Disease Control and Health Prevention]*

Essential oils and aromatherapy techniques may help your efforts to quit smoking. Make your own STOP SMOKING BLEND at home by mixing 5 drops clove oil, 5 drops orange/lemon/lime, 5 drops chamomile, 5 drops helichrysum, 10 drops lavender, 10 drops marjoram and 15 drops grapefruit. Add oils to 10 ml roller ball and top with organic sunflower oil. Roll it on the back of your neck, wrists, and inhale often. This blend is nerve-calming and refreshing.

Inhalation of diffusing black pepper essential oil reduces smoking withdrawal symptoms. Essential oils for smoking work to reduce cravings, lessen anxiety and stress, and ease the nervous system while quitting smoking.

We spend 1/3 of our entire lives in our homes. Air quality, whether you smoke or not, is extremely important to support your respiratory system. Homeowners and renters will go years never cleaning their furnaces. Cleaning your furnace every year is critical for good home air quality. Air filters should be changed every 3-4 months. Turn your furnace into a huge home diffuser by adding 20-30 drops of tea tree or eucalyptus or any of your favourite essential oil on the air filter. Repeat every week for that incredible fresh outdoor scent especially during the long winter months.

Try these helpful hints...

COLD TURKEY

Mix equal parts lemon, black pepper & eucalyptus essential oils.

When you feel the urge to light up a smoke, take a hit of this blend instead.

Inhale deeply. Savor.
Exhale slowly. You got this.

make some QUIT STICKS!

In an 8 oz mason jar (or other flat bottom jar) pour 2 teaspoons fractionated coconut oil. Add 15 drops each cinnamon and black pepper essential oils.

Arrange toothpicks standing up in the jar so all are touching the oil on the bottom. Put the lid on the jar and allow it to stand until the toothpicks soak up all the oil.

Use a toothpick any time the cravings hit!

What Happens When a Smoker QUITS?

Quitting smoking will be hard, as it will affect you mentally and physically, so be prepared for the withdrawal period. But did you know that you will feel the benefits, even just minutes after quitting?

After 20 Minutes... *Blood pressure and heart rate are stabilized.*

After 8 Hours... *Nicotine and carbon monoxide blood levels decrease by half. Oxygen levels normalize and will rejuvenate your skin and hair.*

After 12 Hours... *Carbon monoxide blood levels become normal.*

After 24 Hours... *Carbon monoxide in the blood is expelled. Lungs start clearing off smoking 'debris'.*

After 48 Hours... *Nicotine is completely removed from your body. Your senses get better.*

After 3 days... *Your bronchial tubes let you breathe comfortably. Withdrawal symptoms lead to poor concentration but improved energy levels.*

After 1-2 Weeks... *Lung function and blood circulation improve.*

After 2-12 Weeks... *You may feel irritable and restless. Improved blood circulation gives your skin nutrients that help prevent wrinkles*

After 3-9 Months... *New cell lining (cilia) develop in your lungs to alleviate respiratory problems. Increased appetite.*

After 1 year... *Coronary heart disease risk is cut by half of that of a smoker.*

After 5 Years... *Mouth, throat, esophagus, and bladder cancer risk is half of a smoker. Lower risk of stroke and cervical cancer.*

After 10 years... *Lower risk of pancreatic and larynx cancer. Risk of dying from lung cancer is half of a smoker's.*

After 15 Years... *Your risk of heart disease is the same as that of a non-smoker.*

Evidence based on extensive research studies by the National Toxicology Program of the U.S. Department of Health and Human Services lists alcohol as a known human carcinogen. The more alcohol consumed over time, the higher the risks of developing an alcohol-associated cancer. People who consume 50 or more grams of alcohol per day [approximately 3.5 or more drinks per day] are at a greater risk. Add tobacco to the mix and that risk is substantially higher.

Alcohol consumption is a major risk factor for certain head and neck cancers, particularly cancers of the pharynx [throat] and larynx. Liver cancer [hepatocellular carcinoma has been linked to excessive drinking. One million women studied in the United Kingdom [which included 28,000 women with breast cancer] who had consumed 10 grams of alcohol per day were associated with a 12% increase in the risk of breast cancer. Colorectal cancer risk for people who regularly drink 3.5 drinks or more per day have 1.5 times the risk of developing colorectal cancer than non drinkers.

Drink in moderation, limit your consumption to one or two drinks on occasion. Drinking more than one or two drinks per day can increase your risk to throat, liver, colorectal and breast cancer.

[www.cancerreasearch.org>about-cancer]

[cancerres.aacrjournals.org>section>posterpresentations-tobacco-alcohol]

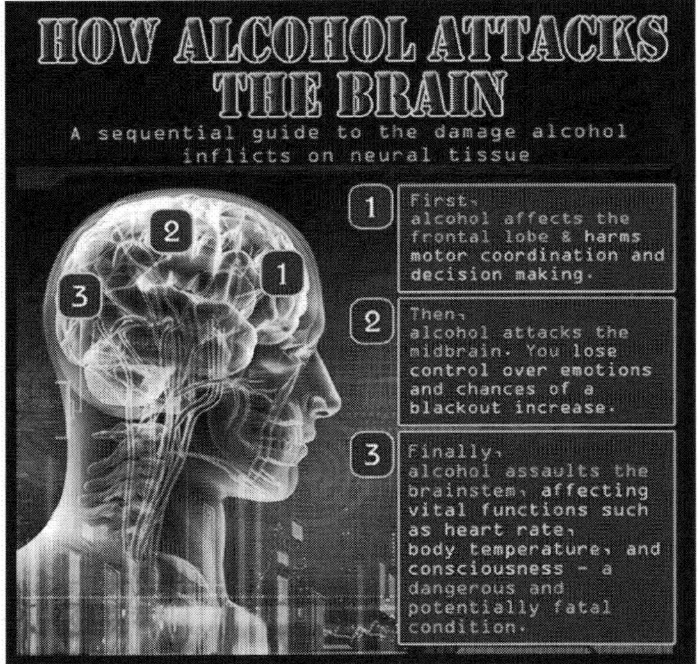

TIPS for Avoiding Relapse

The most important moment before relapse isn't the final decision to use a drug. It's when you decide to expose yourself to triggers. For example, a trigger could be going to a party or walking through the liquor section at the store. Before encountering your triggers, you still have most of the control. Not your craving.

If you're feeling the urge to use, try to wait it out. If you distract yourself for even 30 minutes, it's likely your craving will lessen in intensity. It might not totally disappear, but it will become easier to resist.

Focus on replacing your past drug use with new positive activities. If you used to go home after work and drink, you'll need to make a new plan to occupy yourself. Going home and staring at a wall will eventually lead to staring at a wall with a drink in your hand.

Don't try to do this alone. Sharing your goals for sobriety with a friend makes all the difference. They can hold you accountable when you're making questionable decisions ("I'm just going to the bar to hang out, I won't drink!") and they can offer a kind ear when you're struggling.

Remind yourself that cravings will pass. Have you ever had that experience when you're sick where you can't remember what it feels like to <u>not</u> be sick? The same thing happens with cravings. Give it time, and believe it or not, the feeling will go away.

You'll have to make sacrifices beyond giving up the drug. If you previously used during specific activities (for example: watching a game on TV, going to concerts, or spending time with friends), you may need to make changes. This might mean <u>not</u> watching the game, or making new friends who are sober. This can be really hard, but that's what makes it a sacrifice.

Have a plan for when things get bad, because at some point, they will. People get fired, hearts get broken, and sometimes people leave us forever. Develop a plan to get through these major life challenges - without the use of drugs - before they happen.

Don't become complacent with your sobriety. If you someday consider having "just a glass of wine with dinner", don't make the decision lightly. If you've struggled with addiction in the past, you are much more likely to develop an addiction again.

If you do relapse, don't give up. A lot of people find it helpful to keep track of how long they've been sober, but don't confuse this count with the true goal of leading a good life. If you're at day 100 of sobriety, that's great. However, if you make a mistake and end up back at day 0, know that you are not starting over - you gained knowledge, experience, and confidence. In other words: Slipping up is not a license to go on a binge.

Come up with new rituals. How do you celebrate holidays, promotions, or any other happy occasion? If your answer includes any sort of drug, you'll want to get creative and figure out something new. Go wild with a hobby for the day, treat yourself to a nice dinner, or take a weekend trip. Make sure it's something you can get excited about.

Chapter 4

What Are Essential Oils?

Essential oils are the lifeblood of plants. Their protective internal juices allow them to stay healthy, free of disease, bacteria and outside toxins. This very bloodline of the plant is extracted and just like our blood, helps to oxygenate, regulate, support and heal our bodies.

Oils can be used aromatically, topically and internally (when labelled as a dietary supplement). Always research your essential oil source. The markets are flooded with impure essential oils. They have either been processed by chemical additives such as synthetic perfume or alcohol bases and fillers. Only five percent of essential oil needs to be in a bottle to be able to label it a natural or pure essential oil.

The majority of essential oils on the market are for fragrance (which means chemical-based). When ingesting essential oils, it is critical you know and research your source. We assume that when a bottle says it's 100% pure essential oil, unfortunately, it is not always the case. Also, just because you buy it at a health food store, does not make it pure. Synthetics and chemical additives are known as adulteration of essential oils. It is imperative to your brain, liver, kidney and other body functions to have high-quality essential oil.

Essential oils work very quickly. One drop will fully infiltrate every single body cell with 400,000 molecules in twenty minutes.

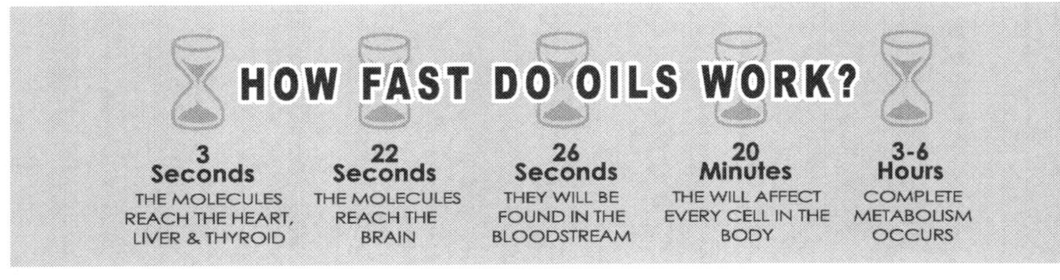

In many of my classes, students ask about allergic reactions to oils. I have never personally seen an allergic reaction to essential oils. Because most allergens are from proteins which are typically one hundred to a thousand times larger than essential oil molecules in both weight and size, there have never been any documented cases of antibody response to the essential oils. Our body reacts to an antigen by our body's immune system formation of antibodies. An antibody must be able to form a protein to cause a reaction. The essential oils are much too small (less than 300 Daltons) so creating a protein is impossible. One of the heaviest essential oils, clary sage, weighs in at 308 Daltons thus their ability to break through the blood-brain barrier. We know that brain cancer is untreatable with chemo therapy because chemo has larger molecules that cannot break the blood-brain barrier.

However, sensitivities to oils can produce a rash, because they are massively detoxifying. Other symptoms include feeling flu-like, overactive sinuses, and headaches. Drink 4-6 glasses of water daily to help flush out toxins, eat healtheir, cut back on coffee, sleep better. These oils are tremendous soldiers on the battlefields, working hard to clear all toxic build-up in your body.

I have witnessed an anxiety attack when one comes close to oil that reminds them of a bad experience with that plant. Breathing deeply with calming oil will settle the reaction in minutes to a positive memory with pleasant sensations.

Applying essential oils topically by way of neat or less diluted oils can cause instant rash or redness. The typical reason a dermal rash will occur is that of the amount of toxicity currently present in the body or perhaps on the skin from heavily concentrated chemical products such as body creams, hand lotions, and other products. The essential oils are doing their job by attacking all the chemicals both inside and outside our bodies, which unfortunately targets our biggest body detoxer, our skin.

Sometimes it's a very good indicator of your gut flora that may be struggling with bacteria overgrowth, or mould toxins.

We found out quickly after my mother used some essential oils 'neat' (undiluted) on her neck and back, she broke out in an itchy rash. After much testing with a functional natural science doctor, we realized she has three annoying moulds in her system that are creating havoc in her system and caused her to be sensitive to more and more food and personal hygiene products. As those moulds are dealt with and chemicals removed from her personal space, she is now able to use essential oils more freely without the outbreaks. It is best to mix oils with a carrier oil and be sure they are adequately diluted.

Both our bodies and essential oils are amazing in that they are always trying to rid us of free radicals raising issues with our immunity and continually bring us back to a neutral zone. They strive to detox and stimulate, so be aware of your body's response and use oils accordingly. Always use carrier oil unless it's a temporary fix that is resolved in one to six weeks, in which case you can use the oils neat. Use oils every day and often throughout the day. When you want results and overall wellness long-term, use essential oils in your deodorant, as your perfume, to sanitize your hands, to ward off colds and flu, in your infused water drinks, cook with them, and most importantly make them a considerable part of your daily lifestyle routine.

Because there are 7,200 nerve endings in our feet, the best place topically to apply your essential oils are to the bottom of your feet which connect to every part of your body. The oils work quickly and efficiently because the bottom of our feet lack sebaceous glands, which therefore allows the oils to penetrate quickly and promptly.

My favourite method of application is to drop some oils in the palm of my hands and clasping them together, rotate clockwise three to four times, inhale deeply for several breaths and then apply to the bottom of my feet using different oils for supporting the different areas of my feet. For example, I might use eucalyptus under my toes for sinus and lung congestion, and use peppermint, fennel, and ginger combination on the stomach and gut areas of my foot. I love changing up my oils because each one has from two hundred to eight hundred properties, so combining them can double and triple your health benefits. I apply, ingest and diffuse oils every single night as well as try to bath in quarter cup natural Epsom and Himalayan salts with eight to ten drops Spruce. I can also use other grounding essential oils to end my day giving my body an opportunity to detox any chemicals and free radicals that I might have encountered in my day.

Ingesting essential oils is hugely beneficial to your gut flora and your body systems. There are several ways to ingest oils, either through the capsule, in a shooter, or through suppositories as done in France.

When I ingest several different oils, I prefer to put them in a one-ounce shooter glass with water. Add drops of essential oils (my family and I use a pure essential oil that I researched and personally visited their farms) plus I like to add a few drops of carrier oil such as coconut, grapeseed, or avocado oil to the mix before I shoot it down. The good fat carrier oils have fantastic health benefits so work well with our keto diets.

Some prefer to put the oils in capsules with the carrier, but I like the quick and easy method.

Always ask the questions. Research the farming practices (no pesticides and herbicides), check your distillation process (no chemicals added), check if they are sourced from third-party brokers, and find out if they own their seeds. Do they bottle their own or are they sourced out? Do they test for purity in-house, or do they use third party testing? Do they purchase other company's sub-par oils? Do they allow you to visit their operations? Do they carry a hundred or more essential oils singles? And more importantly, do they have a certified guarantee for their oils?

The dangers of adulterated oils are real. Today much of the lavender oil in America is a hybrid called lavandin, grown and distilled around the world. Most consumers do not know the difference and happy to buy it for $7 to $10 a bottle. Adulterated and mislabeled essential oils can create dangers to the unsuspecting consumer. For example, lavandin is biologically different than lavender and contains seven to eighteen percent higher levels of camphor that can burn the skin. In contrast, true lavender contains almost no camphor and has burn healing agents not found in lavandin. Adulterated oils are mixed with synthetic extenders such as propylene glycol, DEP or DOP (solvents that have no smell but increase volume). Research your essential oils; each one is very complex in helping take care of your body's natural defence. You want to give it the best natural opportunities without chemical adulteration.

You can go to your government website for a list of essential oils deemed safe to ingest in your drinks, baking or cooking methods.

Always use glass or stainless-steel containers when mixing your essential oils. Always dilute your oils before applying on your skin and avoid personal hygiene products that contain chemicals. Essential oils are known to digest toxic substances, so when they come in contact with chemical residue on the skin, the oils start to work against them.

Research the source of your oils; do your body the best you can with informed decisions.

Safe Dilution for Essential Oils (EO)

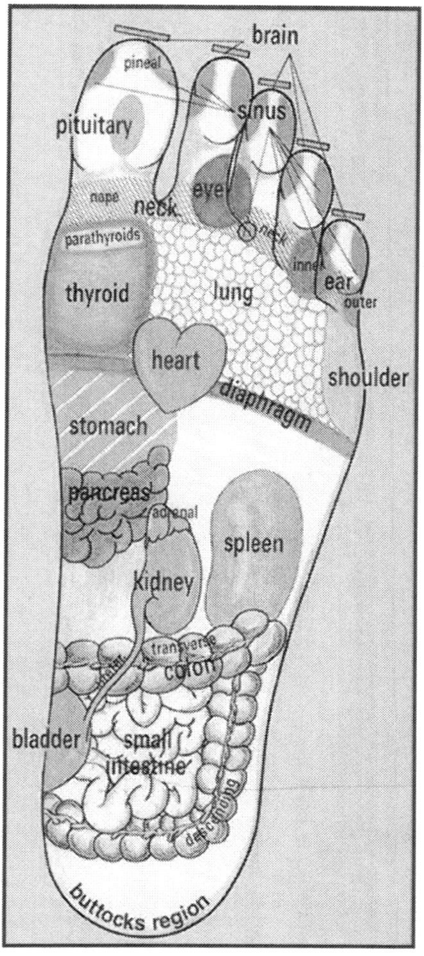

Age/Weight	Recommended Dilution (Total Daily Topical use)
Birth - 1 yr (6-22 pounds)	0.3% dilution (up to 1.5 drops EO)
1 - 5 yrs (23-44 pounds)	1.5% - 3% dilution (up to 15 drops EO)
6 - 11 yrs (45-77 pounds)	1.5% - 5% dilution (up to 17 drops EO)
12 - 17 yrs (78-153 pounds)	1.5% - 20% dilution (up to 25 drops EO)
18 or older (154+ pounds)	1.5% dilution - NEAT (up to 45 drops EO)

Dilution %	Approx. # of EO Drops per tsp Carrier Oil
0.3%	1 drop EO per 2 tsp.
1.5%	2 drops EO per tsp.
3%	3 drops EO per tsp.
5%	5 drops EO per tsp.
10%	10 drops EO per tsp.
20%	20 drops EO per tsp.
33%	33 drops EO per tsp.
50%	50 drops EO per tsp.
NEAT	EO only, no carrier oil

Chapter 5

Carrier Skin Oils That Will Work For You

CARRIER OILS are usually plant-based, extracted from a nut or seed and used to moisturize and heal the skin. These carrier oils are a fabulous way to get your facial skin looking healthy because they give your skin exactly what it wants to help keep it hydrated, moisturized, unclog pores, provides anti-inflammatory properties, help prevent aging and help heal sun damage and age spots.

Other carrier oils are of heavier consistency such as coconut oil, cocoa butter—which should not be used on the face— but is perfect for feet, elbows, knees and legs.

Always buy organic, first cold press and unrefined for best quality of these oils. Natural oils absorb quickly into the skin because they do not contain any added fillers or chemicals. There are many oils that are adulterated with canola oils and cheaper oils to increase production. Research your sources because pure organic oils are best carriers for your skin. Do not shortchange your health by buying less than the best. Carrier oils supplied with pure essential oils will protect your skin from the elements and keep it healthy and glowing.

8 Best Carrier Oils
for Mixing with Pure Essential Oils for Your Skin

1. **RASPBERRY SEED OIL** - its botanical name is Rubus idaeus: is a great moisturizer, anti-inflammatory, and antioxidant for the skin. Raspberry seed oil offers anti-aging benefits of improving skin elasticity, suppleness, flexibility while softening and smoothing the look of wrinkles, fine lines, and sagging skin.

   It absorbs UB-B and UV-C which makes is so useful as a broad-spectrum sunscreen. It is an antioxidant, high in vitamin E, essential to prevent oxidative damage, which can lead to premature skin aging and skin cancer. It is also high in phytosterols that can help reduce trans-epidermal water loss by keeping the skin moisturized and help repair skin damage caused by environmental and chemical factors including sun damage.

2. **CAMELLIA OIL** - is a tea seed oil known as Camellia Sinensis or Camellia Oleifera. It is light green with a mild smell, has a bland flavour, and usually is not used as a cooking oil because it's more expensive than regular oils.

   The leaves of the plant are commonly dried to produce tea; the seeds undergo a cold-pressing extraction to produce the concentrated oil. Camellia oil has many of the same antioxidants compounds as tea and has a high level of unsaturated fats. It also has other minerals that moisturize skin, increase hair health, lowers blood pressure, treats osteoporosis, lowers cholesterol, reduces joint inflammation, boosts immune wound healing, stimulates wound healing and helps prevent cancer. A unique component of camellia oil is squalane, a rare compound believed to have potent anticancer properties, and although research is ongoing, it is firmly considered to be anti-carcinogenic for breast, prostate and colon cancers.

   [http://en.cnki.com.cn/Article_en/CJFDTOTAL-LCH6200601003.htm]

3   **JOJOBA OIL** - is wonderful for all skin types and absorbs into the skin very quickly. Even though it feels like oil, it is a liquid wax ester made from expeller-pressed jojoba seeds. It is very similar to sebum in human skin, and the oil can dissolve sebum and carry healing essential oils deep into the skin. An excellent moisturizer and hydration make it a great carrier oil for body butter, deodorants, lip balm and face oils.

4   **EVENING PRIMROSE OIL** - is an excellent choice for oily and acne-prone skin. The gamma-linoleic acid nutrients in this oil are essential for cell structure and improve the elasticity of the skin. It is incredibly moisturizing, reduces wrinkles, dryness, encourages regeneration of skin cells and keeps skin soft. It can be used to treat skin conditions like eczema, psoriasis, and rosacea.

5   **OLIVE OIL** - extra organic virgin, cold press, unrefined olive oil is one of the oils that are supported by scientific research. Extracted from the fatty fruit of the olive tree, it retains 73% fatty acid (a monounsaturated fat called oleic acid) that has extreme health benefits. Not only great for your skin but a healthy choice for cooking. Unfortunately, much of our olive oil is often adulterated with cheaper chemical laden oils, so it is important to look for organic extra virgin olive oil and research the source to be sure you are getting the real thing.

Olive oil is loaded with powerful antioxidants that can fight inflammation and help cholesterol in our blood from becoming oxidized, both crucial for prevention of heart disease and rheumatoid arthritis. The key antioxidant is oleocanthal, which has been shown to work similarly to ibuprofen, an anti-inflammatory drug. Some scientists estimate that 50 ml (three-quarters of a tablespoon of extra virgin olive oil) has similar effectiveness as 10% of the adult dose of ibuprofen. It not only lowers inflammation but protects LDL cholesterol from oxidation, improves the function of the lining of the blood vessels and could prevent unwanted blood clotting. It has been shown to lower blood pressure and blood pressure meds by 48%. Consuming olive oil does not appear to increase the likelihood of weight gain.

The antioxidants in olive oil can reduce oxidative damage due to free radicals, which is believed to be among the leading drivers of cancer. Many test tube studies have shown that compounds in olive oil can help fight cancer cells. People in Mediterranean countries have a lower risk of some cancers, and many researchers believe olive oil is the prevention.

Because olive oil has antibacterial properties, it can inhibit or kill harmful bacteria. Test tube research has shown extra virgin olive oil to be effective against eight strains of bacteria, three found resistant to antibiotics. A study in humans shows that thirty grams of extra virgin olive oil can eliminate Helicobacter pylori infections in 10%-40% of people in as little as two weeks. This bacterium is known to cause stomach ulcers, gastric, liver, pancreatic duct and gallbladder cancers.

Because of the three main antioxidants in olive oil, Vitamin E, polyphenols and phytosterols, it has huge anti-aging benefits for the skin. Cleopatra bathed in olive oil and was known for the most beautiful skin. Some of the everyday include homemade makeup remover, lip balm, cuticle conditioners, hair treatment, cracked heel and cracked cuticle repair, face cream infused with pure essential oils and hair conditioner. *[Source: International Agency for Research on Cancer, ID: 9283212614]*

6 COCONUT OIL - is high in natural saturated fats, increases the healthy cholesterol (HDL), and also helps covert the LDL (bad cholesterol) into good. By increasing the healthy cholesterol, this helps promote heart health and benefits the heart by lowering high triglycerides. To date over 1,500 studies have been done to prove coconut oil is one of the healthiest foods on the planet. There are three different fats in the oil. Caprylic acid travels directly to your liver to be converted to ketones. The ketone bodies then travel throughout your systems as an alternative energy supply to fuel the nitochondria. Second, lauric acid is known to reduce candida, fight bacteria, and create a hostile environment for viruses.

Third, capric acid has cell binding protection. Coconut oil is composed of about 62% of these three fatty acids in coconut oil. About 91% of the fat is healthy saturated fat which makes it one of the most beneficial fats on the planet. These fats are easy to digest, not readily stored as fat, antimicrobial, antifungal, are smaller in size, allowing easier cell permeability for instant energy and are processed by the liver immediately so are not stored in the body as fat.

Most fats we consume take longer to digest but MCFAs (found in coconut oil) provide an energy source because they only go through the 3-step process to be turned into energy-burning fuel versus other fats that go through a 26-step process. You can replace grains and sugars in your diet with coconut oil as your natural fuel source when you are battling a chronic disease.

Coconut oil has two qualities that help fight cancer. One, the ketones is produced in digestion. Tumour cells are not able to access energy from ketones because they are glucose dependent. Our family is on the ketogenic diet and can attest to this being a huge part of induced, regression on the road to recovery. Tumours have been regressing in size and density as we continue on the functional science health program outlined throughout this information book.

Ketones are made in the liver from fat breakdown, which are then released into the blood to fuel cells like our brains and muscles. This process by which the body burns ketones for fuel, is called ketosis. Your body runs on good fats instead of sugar.

Secondly, as the MCFAs digest the lipid walls of bacteria, they also kill the Helicobacter pylori bacteria known to increase stomach related cancers. Research showed even when cancer was chemically induced, the introduction of coconut oil prevented the cancer from developing.

Also, this super fat is so easy to digest and has been known to improve symptoms of gallbladder disease as well as supporting the pancreas.

Research also shows ketones from coconut oil could create an alternate source of energy to help repair brain function in Alzheimers patients.

Coconut oil has been known to clear and heal urinary tract infections and kidney infections, working as a natural antibiotic by disrupting lipid coating on bacteria and killing them. Coconut oil directly protects the liver from free radical damage.

Because coconut oil is antibacterial, antifungal, and antiviral, it can create a hostile environment for diseases. The oil contains lauric acid, known to reduce Candida.

Taking one tablespoon of coconut oil three times daily, infused with pure essential oils when you are sick, can help you recover quicker. *[Source: Journal Antimicrobial Agents and Chemotherapy]*

Coconut oil helps burn calories, decreases appetite, is helpful in losing belly fat, promotes a healthy digestive process that takes the strain off the pancreas and gives the body a consistent energy source that is not dependant or glucose reactions, which can prevent Type 2 Diabetes. *[Source: 1985 Journal of Toxicology and Environmental Health; Obesity Research Journal - Boston University Medical School]*

According to recent findings written in the Medical Journals Food and Function, coconut oil improves antioxidant levels and can slow aging. It works by reducing stress on the liver and lowering oxidative stress. To naturally slow aging, take one tablespoon of coconut oil with antioxidant-rich berries for breakfast or add to your smoothie. Apply to your skin, although not recommended for your face as it can cause acne for some, but excellent for the bottom of your feet, elbows, legs, and buttocks especially when infused with pure essential oils. Use it as a face cleanser and is excellent for skin conditions such as psoriasis, eczema, and rough, dry skin patches.

Be sure to research your sources. Refined or processed coconut oil can be bleached. Buy organic, extra virgin, cold pressed and unrefined. For seventy-seven more coconut oil uses and cures, check out www.daxe.com.

7 **SHEA BUTTER** - has a substantial healing fraction, which sets it apart from other seed oils. Depending on the source, the healing fraction of shea butter ranges from 5%-17%, in comparison to other seed oils that are in the range of 1%.

It nourishes the skin with vitamin A, A-E and F (essential fatty acids) easily penetrates the skin and will not clog pores. Vitamins A and E maintain the skin by keeping it clear and healthy, help prevent premature wrinkles and facial lines, help repair sun damaged skin, and help improve skin conditions including blemishes, eczema, and dermatitis. Vitamin F is the protector and rejuvenator, soothing dry or damaged skin, and has properties to treat skin allergies, insect bites, sunburn and frostbite.

There is a high level of cinnamic acid, allowing shea butter to be a natural sunscreen. Its anti-inflammatory properties make it useful in treating arthritis. Because shea butter's properties are similar to those produced by our sebaceous glands, it is by far one of the skin's all-time favourite moisturizer and hydrator. (Note: buy organic, unrefined, and first cold press)

8 **SAFFLOWER OIL** - contains about 78% linoleic acid which is undoubtedly a secret weapon in fighting against acne. Other benefits include its ability to lower cholesterol levels, manage blood sugar, aid in weight loss, reduce PMS symptoms, and improve the immune system.

The high content of linoleic acid in safflower oil makes it ideal for boosting the quality and appearance of your skin. The linoleic acid can combine with sebum to unclog pores, reduce blackheads and acne which is a result of build-up of sebum under the skin. It also stimulates the regeneration of new skin cells to help clear up scars and other blemishes.

Allergic to ragweed? You might want to avoid safflower, as it's from the same botanical family.

Chapter 6

Essential Oils and Cancer Research

No matter how compliant rules are about the dangers of prescription drugs, deaths and damages occur. According to the Centres for Disease Control and Prevention, more than 100,000 Americans die every year from properly prescribed, properly taken prescriptions.

The molecules of pharmaceutical drugs are all strange to the human body. Hence the body does not efficiently metabolize them. On the other hand, natural molecules such as those found in pure essential oils, are quickly metabolized by the body. When an essential oil molecule finds the receptor sites it was designed to fit and conveys its information to the cell, or paricipates in other therapeutic functions, it then goes on its way to the liver and kidneys and moves out of the body. Its benefits have been conveyed and its job complete.

By contrast, the unnatural molecules of human-made drugs attach themselves to various tissues, disrupting normal cell function while the body tries to figure out what to do with them. In the meantime, they wreak mischief with our bodily functions, cause side effects sometimes worse than the issue itself and can stay in our fatty tissues for years - including in our brain.

More research is being conducted on natural therapies, and it is becoming apparent that conventional practices like chemotherapy and radiation are no longer needed to eradicate cancer. In some cases, both have failed patients miserably, sending them to their only other alternative - Functional natural health science. Drugs and oils work in opposite ways. Drugs toxify and essential oils detoxify. Drugs clog and confuse receptor sites, and essential oils clean receptor sites. Drugs depress the immune system, and essential oils strengthen the immune system. Antibiotics attack bacteria indiscriminately, killing both good and bad bacteria while essential oils attack only the harmful bacteria allowing our body's floral to flourish. Essential oils are multi-dimensional, filled with homeostatic intelligence to restore the body to a state of healthy balance. When the body conditions change, oils adapt, raising or lowering blood pressure as needed, stimulating or repressing enzyme activity as required, and energizing or relaxing the body as needed. Because essential oils, when correctly applied, always work toward restoration of proper bodily function; they do not cause undesirable side effects.

Essential oils, supplements, chemical-free living, diet, exercise, yoga and other modalities are giving many a new lease on life. There are thousands upon thousands of orcinary everyday people claiming that a combination of natural health therapies cured them. Because they are not part of a research study, their testimonies are just that - testimonies. Neverthe ess, they are real, and they are encouraging.

It is a complete lifestyle change that I recommend, not only to cancer patients but for prevention of cancer. Research strongly suggests that oils not only prevent but trect cancer and its debilitating side effects. It's important to remember the increasing numbers of success stories researchers have experienced in using essential oils to prevent and stop or reverse the growth of various cancers in animal and human cell studies. Although the vast majority are based out of Petri dishes; the testimonies online are real-time cancer survivors with real stores of survival and bravery.

Here are examples of research done by doctors, chemists, and aromatherapists:

"Our bodies are biologically programmed to react to essential oil constituents, which interact with a variety of receptor sites, neurochemicals and enzymes, giving them the potential for therapeutic activity."
- **Robert Tisserand**

"Essential oils promote natural healing by stimulating and reinforcing the body's mechanisms. Essences of chamomile and thyme, for instance, are credited with the ability to stimulate the production of white blood cells which help in our fight against the disease."
- **Chrissie Wildwood, 1991**

"Essential oils include muscle relaxants, digestive tonics, circulatory stimulants and hormone precursors. Many repair injured cells, while others carry away metabolic waste. Also, some essential oils enhance immunity, working with the body to heal itself. They are capable of stimulating the production of phagocytes (white blood cells that attack invaders)."
- **Kerville and Green, 1995**

"What do oils do? They transport fuel to our cells, they normalize the viscosity of the blood and facilitate the delivery of vital nutrients. They release toxins, clean the gallbladder and stimulate the secretion of gastric juices. Essential oils were used as traditional medicines, were historically used in spiritual ceremonies and also used by ancient people for survival. Essential oils are the intelligence of the plants."
- **Cole L. Woolley, PhD**

"Essential oils are the regenerating and oxygenating immune defence properties of plants. They bring life to plants, destroying infections, starving off infestation, aiding in growth and stimulate healing. They are to plants what blood is to the human body plus so much more."
- **D. Gary Young, 1995**

"Using cancer cell apoptosis induction trials, previous studies of myrrh and frankincense essential oils are capable of inducing cancer cell apoptosis. For example, sesquiterpenes have anti-cancer cells in the G0/G1 phase."
- **Yingli Chen, et al., College of Pharmacy, Harbin Medical University, Daquin, China, 2013**

"Boswellia Sacra (SACRED Frankincense from Oman and Yemen) essential oil induces breast cancer cell-specific cytotoxicity. Suppression of cellular network formation and disruption of spheroid development of breast cancer cells by Boswellia Sacra essential oil suggest that the oil may be effective for advanced breast cancer. Consistently, the essential oil represses signalling pathways and cell regulators that have been proposed as therapeutic targets for breast cancer."
- **Mahmoud M Suhail, et al., Al Aria Medical Complex, Salalah Sultanate of Oman, 2011**

Chapter 7

The Science Behind Aromatherapy

Aromatherapy is the inhalation and topical application of essential oils (or the pure essence of plants). As a form of alternative medicine, it is used to enhance physical, mental, emotional and spiritual well-being.

Let's take a look at the general health benefits of aromatherapy:

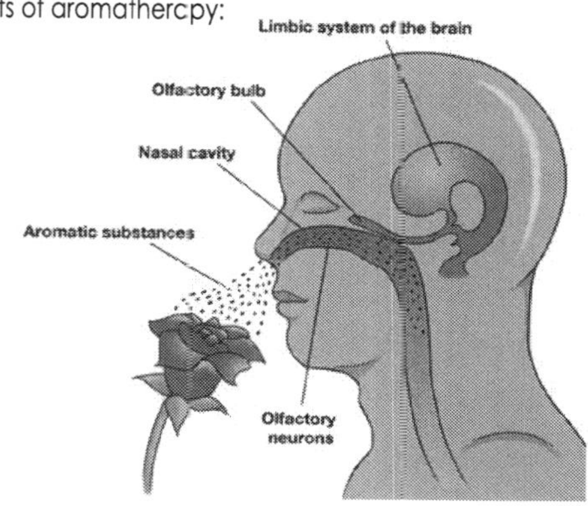

Inhalation

When a person inhales an essential oil, that scent is carried by olfactory nerve cells in the nose to the olfactory system which then sends the aroma to the brains limbic system, the house of emotions and emotional behaviours such as intimacy, passion and sex. Immediately, and depending on the oil, you may begin to feel more alert or more relaxed. You may feel excited and aroused. You may feel the release of negative emotions and the soothing of muscle tension. Mood enhancers like serotonin and endorphins get released.

Our sense of smell is 10,000 times more potent than any other sense, and the recognition of smell is immediate (other senses like touch travel to the brain via the spinal cord). Smell is also the most active link to the subconscious mind and even to our collective unconscious mind where memories are stored.

'Positive Energy Diffuser'
4 drops Bergamot
4 drops Orange
3 drops Eucalyptus

Topical Application

Essential oils have high antioxidant properties as measured by the Oxygen Radical Absorbance Capacity (ORAC), a test developed by the U.S. Department of Agriculture and Tufts University to measure the antioxidant speed and power of free radical inhibition. The oxidative damage caused by free radicals is implicated in everything, from aging and wrinkling of skin to DNA damage, cancer, heart disease, and premature death. Antioxidants control for free radical damage at the cellular level and support youthful aging and a healthy body.

While vegetables and fruits have antioxidant power (e.g.- cucumber at sixty units of antioxidant strength; celery at seventy-five units; apple at 207 units; broccoli at 890 units; blueberries at 2,400 units), essential oils have higher antioxidant power (orange oil at 18,898 units, ylang ylang has an

ORAC of 1,300,478 units, patchouli has an approximate ORAC of 494,271 units). *["Units" are actually called "TE/L." TE/L is expressed as micromole Trolox equivalent per liter]*

When essential oils are applied to the skin, the oils are absorbed through the skin. Since the oils don't dissolve in water and attach to body fat and fluids, they get into the body's systems, bringing their antioxidants and enhancing our immune strength.

Why Aromatherapy Boosts Mood! FEEL THE VIBE...

In addition to the antioxidant influx that essential oils bring when applied to the skin, the oils also invoke good feelings of wellness and vitality through a process called "entrainment." According to researchers in Washington using Tainio Technology, the vibrational frequency of essential oils is the highest of any natural substance known to man. Through the principle of entrainment, the oil's higher frequency will raise the vibratory quality of that individual.

For example, their technology has shown these frequencies:

- healthy human body is 62-70 MHz
- human cells can start to change (mutate) when their frequency drops below 62MHz
- 58 MHz is the frequency of your body when you have a cold or the flu
- when candida is present within your body, you vibrate at a frequency of 55MHz
- 52 MHz is the frequency of a body with Epstein-Barr virus present
- 42 MHz is the frequency of a body wherein cancer can appear. When the death process begins, the frequency has been measured at 20 MHz

The measured frequencies of essential oils have been shown to go as high as 320 MHz as seen with rose oil! Lavender has a frequency of 118 MHz, and sandalwood has a frequency of 96 MHz. Oils entrain the cells of the body to increase their vibratory rate. Can you feel the vibe of good health? Good health has a frequency of 70MHz.

To put this frequency business into perspective, dead foods such as hamburger and chicken have a frequency of 3 to 5 MHz; raw almonds vibrate at 50 MHz, living greens such as broccoli and wheatgrass have a frequency of 70MHz. Living greens, herbs and botanicals capture light from the sun and that light or "life force" is held in the molecules.

Energy

Albert Einstein said it best when he said: "Everything is energy." We live in a sea of vibration! Four out of our five senses - sight, sound, touch, and taste - receive sensory data from the environment which is transferred through the nervous system to the brain. At the brain level, data is interpreted based on our mental schemas or mental filters (i.e.- beliefs). For example, when a person hears a dog barking, that bark is a sound vibration that the ears receive, and then they send that signal to the brain where the person perceives the sound to be from a dog. If the person initially "learned" that bark was from a cat then he would interpret the sound data according to that belief system.

Aroma (smell)

Scents trigger an area in the brain called the Limbic System.

When stimulated, it releases endorphins, neurotransmitters and other feel-good chemiclas.

This can be achieved by direct inhalation or diffusion.

When it comes to the sense of smell, an odor is received by the receptors in the nose, and that signal is transferred to the olfactory bulb which is part of the limbic brain. Because smell data doesn't need first travel to the nervous system and instead goes directly to the brain, it is said that smell is the brain's direct link to the environment. All smells, like all sounds, for example, have their signature frequency. If they didn't have their vibration, we wouldn't be able to tell one odour from the other scent.

Since the human body is energy, it makes sense to use energy based products that are in alignment with us to support our body and mind. We have the human body, then we have organs that make up the human body, then we have cells that make up the organs, then we have atoms that are the blueprint for the cells, and at the subatomic level there are electrons, vortexes of energy. Science shows what Einstein said, "Everything is energy, including humans."

When it comes to the botanical essences of aromatherapy, their natural ability to enhance our health and well-being are without a doubt in alignment with our vibrational nature.

Peppermint aromatherapy has been found to increase memory and alertness. Researchers at the University of Northumbria in the U.K. had 144 volunteers take cognitive tests and complete a mood evaluation while being exposed to either peppermint, ylang ylang or no aroma. The peppermint group scored better on alertness and memory tests than the other two groups.

*Some research has shown that **lemon oil** may possess anti-depressant-type effects, making it a good choice for stress relief and mood enhancement as well. Japanese scientists studied the effect of lemon essential oil on the ability to focus. They discovered that the typical mistakes were reduced by 54 percent when lemon oil was diffused in the work room.*

***Rosemary** is associated with feelings of contentment. It's been shown to have positive effects on performance and mood. In ancient Greece and Rome, wreathes made of Rosemary were worn by students to improve mental focus and memory when studying or taking exams.*

*A randomized study by Wilkinson looked at the effects of massage with or without **chamomile** on 51 patients with cancer. The results of this study showed a reduction in tension, anxiety, and pain that was statistically significant.*

Essential Oils and Pharmaceuticals Compared

Essential Oils	Pharmaceuticals
Properties	**Properties**
1. natural, wildcrafted or grown organically	1. unnatural, synthetic chemically or gentically engineered
2. hundreds of constituents, not all known	2. one or two active ingredients, all of which are known
3. never two batches the same	3. every batch the same (purity)
4. not patentable (God made)	4. patentable (man made)
Effects and Consequences	**Effects and Consequences**
5. restores natural function	5. inhibits natural function
6. no adverse interaction	6. many adverse interactions
7. anti-viral	7. usually not anti-viral
8. improves intercellular communication	8. disrupts intercellular communication
9. corrects and restores proper cellular memory (DNA)	9. garbles and confuses cellular memory (DNA)
10. cleanses receptor sites	10. blocks receptor sites
11. builds the immune system	11. depresses immune system
12. emotionally balancing	12. emotionally unbalancing
13. side effects beneficial	13. side effects harmful
14. leads toward independence and wellness	14. leads toward dependence and chronic disease
Philosophy/Paradigm	**Philosophy/Paradigm**
15. assumes wellness as natural state, invulnerable to illness	15. assumes natural state prone and vulnerable to illness
16. assumes body and mind capable of self-healing	16. assumes body and mind need external assistance to heal
17. integrated wholistically, body, mind and soul as a unit	17. fragmented, treats body parts, mind and emotions separate
18. build natural defenses and let body deal with disease	18. supplant natural defenses and attack disease itself
19. treats internally at level of cellular intelligence	19. treats externally at level of gross symptoms

Essential Oil Benefits
for Cancer and Immunity

According to Canadian Cancer Society an estimated 206,200 new cases of cancer and 80,000 deaths will occur in Canada alone in 2017. Half of all new cases will be lung, breast and prostate cancers. Statistics say 1 in 2 Canadians will develop cancer in their lifetimes , 1 in 4 will die of the disease and 60% of Canadians with cancer will survive at least 5 years after diagnosis.

Breast cancer is one of the top five cancers most diagnosed. There is growing evidence that essential oils could play a major role in prevention of breast cancer.
[https://the truthaboutcancer.com>citrus-essential-oils-for-cancer-prevention]

In 2013, the University of Leicester funded by the Omani government funded research uncovered that frankincense has the ability to target cancer cells in late -stage ovarian cancer patients. This appears to be because of AKBA (acetyl-11-keto-boswellic acid). According to ead researcher Kamla Al Salmani, "After a year of studying the AKBA compound with ovarian cancer cell lines in vitro, we have been able to show it is effective at killing cancer cells. Frankincense is taken by many people with no known side effects. This finding has enormous potential to be taken to a clinical trial in the future and developed into an additional treatment for ovarian cancer."

Online testimonies suggest that the amount of B-elemene that frankincense and myrrh contain could very well explain why so many people claim that both o ls have been instrumental to them beating cancer God's way.

Current research demonstrates antimutagenic and apoptotic (programmed cell death) abilities. Though the results have occurred in lab tests and we have yet to see how to best replicate these results in active cancer in humans, the demonstrated results remain. Studies continue to emerge, demonstrating similar effects on bladder, breast, and skin cancers.

There is so much research on essential oils and cancer prevention and can be very effective in ingesting or applying topically in combination with other therapies.

A search of PubMed [http:/www.pubmed.gov/], the National Institute of Health's online research, shows 543 results for the search "cancer essential oils" as of February 2014. Further screening of thesis research papers, nearly 135 correspond to anticancer properties of essential oils. Essential oils from different plants have been reported to have anticancer potential against mouth, breast, lung, prostate, liver cancer, brain, and leukemia cancers. [28.Zu Y, Yu H, LIANG L ,et al. Activities of ten essential oils towards Propionibacterium acnes and PC-3, A-549 and MCF-7 cancer cells. Molecules. 2010;15(5): 3200-3210.] [pubMed] [Ref List]

Dozens of different essential oils can have properties that can help cancer patients in many ways; for relaxation, stress relief, pain relief and overall well being. Massage with essential oils is very powerful especially over the spine, brain stem and vita flex points on the bottom of the feet. Our family are using essential oils consistently everyday for preventive measures and in battling cancer. We ingest oils, diffuse oils, bathe in oils and massage oils.

We are definitely Oilers for life.

#essentialoils   *#oilersforlife*   *#diffuseoils*   *#onedropatatime*

Know your oils and always consult with your health professionals. Read "Essential Oils Desk Reference Book, 6th Edition.

[https://drericz.com/2015/10/diy-essential-oil-protocol-for-cancer-patients /]
[http://thetruthaboutcancer.com/testimonials]

Ledum

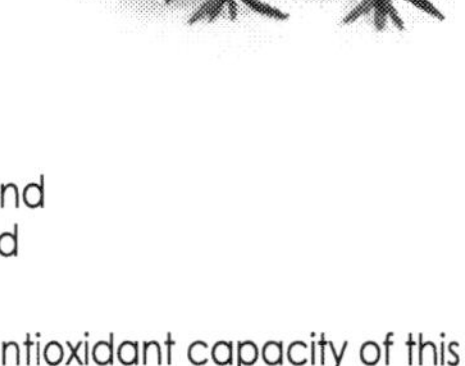

- derived from the leaves of the ledum plant, or more commonly known as Labrador Tea, which is native to the northern hemisphere and recognized for its medicinal benefits for hundreds of years
  [http://en.cnki.com.cn/Article_en/CJFDTOTAL-DBLY701.011.htm]
- great for calming nerves and lowering anxiety levels, it can directly affect the behaviour of the limbic system, the brain's emotional centre, promoting peaceful feelings and general calm, especially when you are feeling overwhelmed
  [http://www.sciencedirect.com/science/article/Pi/SO3788741090041031]
- early studies on ledum and cancer tumours show that the antioxidant capacity of this oil can help eliminate free radicals which can lead to mutation of healthy cells and a higher risk of tumour cells

[http://en.cnki.com.cn/Article_en/CJFDTOTAL-SPKX201219020.htm]

Clary Sage

Due to the content of sclareol (a fragrant chemical compound found in clary sage) that is said to be structurally similar to human estrogens, it impacts cancer by killing, through a process known as apoptosis.

- has interesting anti-cancer activity including in vitro activity against human breast cancer
- inhibits the growth of breast and uterine cancer in vitro
- Apoptosis triggers the call to commit "suicide" – cell death which suggests clary sage could have profound effects on prevention and treatment of cancer
- it contains phytoestrogens which are now commonly avoided with estrogen inducted cancers
- hopefully, further research will reshape the current medical theory the phytoestrogens feed into (in theory) cancers
- based on structures, sclareol is unlikely to have any estrogenic actions
- cell growth inhibitory action of an unusual labdane diterpene, 13-epi-sclareolis also present in clary sage oil, inhibits the growth of breast and uterine cancers in vitro and was slightly more potent than Tamoxifen, but not toxic to healthy cells

[https://breastcancerconquer.com/.]
[Citation Phytother Res.2014 Nov 28(11):1599-605.doi:10.1002/per.5163 EPub 2014 May 7]

Frankincense

- research as recent as 2013-2016 proven to be cytotoxic to the ovarian cancer cells
- ½ teaspoon a day – in a trial in 2011 given to 44 patients with Brain cancer – reduced swelling by 75% in 60% of participants
- helps manage depression, pain and boost immune
- found frankincense is not just a supplemental treatment to go alongside chemo and radiation, but in some cases, it's maybe preferential and a replacement when chemo is not an option
- related research shows frankincense is effective against other forms of cancer including breast, colon and prostate; Doctors in this research explained certain cancer cell lines do not respond to chemo are notably responsive to Frankincense

[http://www.ncbi.nim.nih.gov/pic/articles/PMC 3258268]
[http://www.ncbbi.ncbi.nim.nih.gov/pic/articles PMC3924999/]

Lavender

- eliminates free radicals created by chemicals, pollutants, stress and toxins form cellular damage, immune inhibition and chronic diseases including cancer
- free radicals are Super Villains – Antioxidants are Super Heroes
- lavender is a useful natural antioxidant supplement, merely inhaling one hour each day suggests neuroprotective anti-poptolic activities help against stress in the brain

[www.thetruthaboutcancer.com]

Lemongrass

- in vitro cytotoxicity ability against twelve human cancer cell lines, researchers discovered that essential oil triggers a variety of mechanisms that kill cancer cells
- oil research shows promising anti-cancer activity and causes the loss in tumour cell viability by activating the apoptotic process as identified by electron microscopy

[http://www.cancer.gov/cancertopics/pdq/cam/aromatherapy/healthproffessional]
National Cancer Institute "Aromatherapy and Essential Oils (PDQ)

Myrrh

- myrrh plus frankincense relieves swelling and pain, exhibit synergistic effects on harmful bacterial infections - Cryptococcus, neoformans and pseudomonas
- due to its anti-oxidant properties, it can alleviate all dangerous bacteria that typically infect airways, urinary tract, burns and blood infections, usually require treatments
- lab-based study found myrrh has anti-cancer benefits, inhibiting growth in eight different types of cancer, specifically gynecological cancers

[http:www.academicjournals.org/JMPR] ISSN 1996-0875-2011 Academic Journals

Peppermint & Spearmint

- effective for treatment of nausea and vomiting while undergoing chemo
- mouthwash – eucalyptus, melaleuca, lemongrass, lemon, clove and thyme for metastatic tumorigenic ulcers of the skin

Thyme

- used to induce cell death in breast cancer cells; after 72 hours of treatment, thyme essential oil killed 98% of human breast cancer cells
- is a promising candidate in development of the drugs for breast cancer
- may be beneficial against prostate, lung carcinoma and breast cancers
- thymol which makes up 20-50% of thyme oil is known as the biocide, which means it can destroy harmful organisms and gives thyme oil strong antimicrobial properties
- strong antibacterial properties and according to a study at the Society for Generic Microbiology in Edinburgh pointed out that essential oils may be effective and affordable alternatives to antibiotics in a battle against resistant bacteria

[http://www.ncbi.nim.nihgov/pic/articles/PMC4070586]

Citrus Oils

- lime, lemon, orange, grapefruit, tangerine – now have over 200 research studies on limonene discussing anti-cancer benefits
- limonene content in citrus essential oils:
    - lemon essential oil...... 59-73% limonene
    - lime essential oil...... 50-60% limonene
    - orange essential oil...... 85-96% limonene
    - tangerine essential oil...... 85-93% limonene
    - grapefruit essential oil...... 88-95% limonene

- other phytochemicals found in citrus essential oils include perillyl alcohol, alphapenene, seta pinene myrcene; all of these phytochemicals have been researched as having potent anti-cancer activity; the most studied phytochemical is limonene
- about 1,000 lemons yield one pound of lemon essentia oil; it takes 75 lemons to make 15 ml of lemon essential oil
- put 3-5 drops of citrus fresh in morning water for anti-cancer and excel ent liver detox
- cancer patients undergoing chemo can use citrus oils to help speed healing process of mouth ulcers; rub a drop of lemon, lime, tangerine, ar orange essential oil onto the affected area of your mouth; repeat as often as needed for relief
- improve breast health by messaging the breast daily with a combination of your favourite citrus essential oils, frankincense, lavender and sandalwood
- in 2015 a study on human pancreatic cancer cells in vitro (test tubes) found limonene promotes apoptosis (programmed all death cancer cells)
- limonene inhibits the growth of cancer cells
- rinse your fruit with citrus essential oils and expand their shelf life
- drinks infused with citrus essential oils last up to seven days

[https://thetruthaboutcancer.com>citrus-essential-oils-for-cancer-prevention]

In conclusion, of all studies and research in medical literature this is just a sample of those that suggest essential oils for cancer therapy can benefit patients. These oils car be diffused, diluted and applied topically to the affected area, used in therapeutic bath, or applied in massgae therapies.

If you are taking chemo, it does not mean you can't use oils; far too many oncclogists do not give enough emphasis on the practicality of using both togetr er.

Most reviewed articles we have that evaluate the ability of essential oils for cancer to prevent, and even reverse the growth of various malignant lines are in vitro. In other words, we do not have human trials, but what we do have are thousands upon thousands cf testimonials of people on the internet claiming essential oils cured them of cancer. This information cannot be disputed by me as I have a miracle happening in my son's life. These oils are his lifeline.

Always consult with your physician or health professional. Essential oils should be safety administrated according to dilution charts and instructions. These statements have not been evaluated by the FDA. These products are not intended to ciagnose, treat, cure or prevent any disease.

Favourite Roller Ball Recipes for Cancer Patients & Survivors

Add high grade essential oils to a 10 ml roller ball, then top with carrier oil such as organic sunflower, camellia, jojoba, or your favourite choice.

Life / Love / Hope in Healing

This combo helps to align the spine and balances the emotional and structural body, targets the pathogens on the spine, helps with blood circulation and fluid retention, helps with muscular, joint and all types of pain, helps with muscular spasms, stressed muscles, fatigue and helps promote better sleep and calm.

peaceful: calm: balance: heal: focus: grounded: revitalize

10 drops SPRUCE - *grounds the body, releases emotional blocks and beneficial for bone pain, aching joints, stimulating the thymus and adrenal glands*

15 drops FRANKINCENSE - *the Holy oil, the king of oils is anti-catarrhal, anti-cancer, anti-depressant, anti-infectious, anti-inflammatory, antiseptic, anti-tumoral, immune stimulant and sedative*

5 drops BLUE TANSY - *helps cleanse the liver and calm the lymphatic system to help rid oneself of anger and promote a feeling of self control*

5 drops ROSE - *helps prevent scarring, relieves headaches and nervous tension, liver congestion, poor circulation and helps to stimulate and elevate the mind, creating a sense of well being*

10 drops BASIL - *anti-viral, decongestant of arteries of the lungs, veins and prostate, stimulates the nerves, adrenal cortex, energizes and is restorative*

8 drops CYPRESS - *helps with circulation and fluid retention, lymphatic and prostate decongestant, supports the liver and respiratory systems; it creates a feeling of security, grounding and helps to heal emotions*

10 drops CEDARWOOD - *is protecting, recharging, rejuvenating, calms anger and helps with anxiety*

10 drops LEDUM - *anti-cancerous, anti-mutagenic, anti-tumoral, nerve stimulant, powerful liver support and detoxifier, can support inflamed lymph nodes and help thyroid regulation*

5 drops LAVENDER - *anti-mutagenic, anti-depressant, anti-tumour, regenerative and calming; known to balance the body and to work wherever there is a need to promote consciousness, health, love and peace*

10 drops WINTERGREEN - *muscular pain, cortisone-like action, hypertension, inflammation, and known for its ability to alleviate bone pain due to a high content of methyl salicylate*

10 drops LEMON - *beneficial for anxiety, improving clarity of thought, helps with red blood cell formation, memory improvement, reduces stress, anti-cancer, anti-depressant, invigorating and refreshing*

There are many essential oils that can support you during treatment and as a preventive and post cancer protocol. This combination of oils has some of nature's best and together can support all body functions. You can apply the rollerball to the spine, bottom of your feet, over the area affected, back of your neck and to your wrists.

Oils are absorbed by your body quickly to rejuvenate, rebuild and support cell structure. Apply often, three to five times a day initially, and can be reduced as your body strengthens. Morning and bedtime are favoured times for application.

As always, check with your health professional and take the best choices for you.

Pain & Calm

relief: sooth: calm: energize: balance

30 drops SPRUCE

30 drops WINTERGREEN

25 drops PALO SANTO - *anti-tumoral, immune stimulant, helps with muscle pain and promotes spiritual awareness*

20 drops HELICHRYSUM - *helps to cleanse the blood and improve circulatory functions and is anti-inflammatory*

20 drops VETIVER - *calming, psychologically grounding, calming, stabilizing properties, immune-stimulant, rubefacient, stimulant of circulatory and production of red corpuscles, and effective for emotional balance; it is valuable for relieving stress and helping people recover from emotional trauma and shock; as a natural tranquilizer, it can induce a restful sleep*

15 drops FRANKINCENSE

15 drops COPAIBA - *helpful for muscle aches, inflammation, pain, is anti-inflammatory, supports poor circulation, stiffness and acts like a kicker to other oils escalating the effectiveness of all oils*

10 drops ROSEMARY - *anti-cancer, anti-fungal, anti-inflammatory, anti-infectious, stimulates the immune system, prevents respiratory infections, candida, other infections like staph & strep*

10 drops MARJORAM - *helpful for fluid retention, muscle spasms, stiff joints, relaxing and calming and can help with anxiety*

8 drops LEMONGRASS - *anti-cancer, anti-bacterial, anti-inflammatory, revitalizer, helpful for regenerating connective tissue, lymphatic drainage, regulates parasympathetic nervous system and strengthens vascular walls*

5 drops CLOVE - *anti-tumoral, anti-bacterial, anti-fungal, anti-inflammatory, anti-infectious, anti-viral, and immune stimulant. Rinse to speed healing of mouth sores caused by chemo; influences healing, improves memory, initiates a good nights sleep and inhibits tumours and skin cancer*

Chemotherapy side effects can be horrendous and frightful. Often while the chemotherapy treatment takes place, your oncologist may suspend the use of the oils.

Chemo is generally out of your system in hours but the side effects can linger for 6 months to a year after treatment. It can take 21 to 28 days for your immune to recover on its own merit. Essential oil blends like these two can be very helpful to suppress the side effects and help the damaged good cells to heal quicker. They also support the immune system and protect against viral and bacterial infections. High grade essential oils are a powerhouse in the battle against cancer when western medicine is not an option.

Diffusing Oil Combinations for Cancer Patients

DIFFUSERS come in a variety of styles and options, light features and timer settings. Choose one that is CSA approved and is capable of withstanding pure essential oils. If the plastics they are made from are carcinogenic, the oils will destroy the chemical components of the diffuser.

Anger Management

stay calm: grounded: relaxed: happy

4 drops BERGAMOT
2 drops LAVENDER
2 drops FRANKINCENSE
2 drops SPRUCE
1 drop JUNIPER

Stay Calm & Focused

relax: peaceful: balance: grounded: focus

3 drops VETIVER
3 drops CEDARWOOD
2 drops SANDALWOOD
2 drops LAVENDER
1 drop MARJORAM

Memory Loss / Brain Fog

alert: focus: memory: uplift: at peace: joy: balance

4 drops ROSEMARY
4 drops FRANKINCENSE
2 drops PEPPERMINT
2 drops ORANGE
2 drops LIME

Depression / Anxiety

peaceful: balanced: grounded: at ease

4 drops FRANKINCENSE
3 drops LAVENDER
2 drops VETIVER
2 drops JASMINE
2 drops BERGAMOT

Immune Boosters 1 & 2

powerful anti-viral: anti-bacterial

3 drops SPRUCE
3 drops LEMON
2 drops EUCALYPTUS
2 drops CLOVES
2 drops ROSEMARY

3 drops MARJORAM
3 drops LAVENDER
3 drops PEPPERMINT
2 drops CINNAMON BARK
2 drops BLACK PEPPER

Sleepy Time

relaxed: sleepy: calm: content

4 drops RUTAVALA
2 drops SPRUCE
2 drops FRANKINCENSE
2 drops VETIVER
2 drops PATCHOULI

Diffuser recipes can be converted to a 10 ml roller ball - just fill bottle with carrier oil and add essential oil drops. Apply to back of neck, wrists and inhale often throughout the day.

Chapter 9

Thirteen More Support Therapies for Cancer and Chronic Disease

Many modalities can help you achieve optimum body health. It's super important to maintain body detox, muscle building, and healthy heart functions. Here is a dozen more ways to care for yourself.

INFRARED SAUNA or having accessibility to one is crucial. A group of Finnish researchers at the University of Eastern Finland in Kuopio uncovered health benefits using saunas. A study published in JAMA Internal Medicine monitored the sauna-going habits of 2,315 middle-aged men and found those who sauna-bathed regularly reduced their overall risk of cardiovascular disease by removing toxins, improving blood vessel function, and optimizing overall cardiovascular health.

Men in the study who enjoyed the sauna two to three times per week reduced their chances of heart-related death by 27% and those who went seven days a week reduced it by 50% compared to those who visited the sauna only once a week.

Sauna bathing can trigger the eccrine glands to secrete a quart of perspiration in just fifteen minutes. It cools the body and rids it of harmful waste products like environmental pollutants, man-made chemicals in the water, air, solvents, pesticides, prescription drugs, nicotine, and alcohol.

Dr. Luke Fortney, Assistant Professor of Family Medicine and Public Health at the University of Wisconsin, recommends the sauna to his patients to help regulate blood pressure. It is considered safer than prescription medication in the treatment of anxiety disorders, seasonal affective disorder, joint pain and for soothing muscle spasms.

Another study by Sydney Ziverts, a health and nutrition investigator for www.consumersafety.org, investigated infrared saunas and says science shows real benefits to infrared sauna therapy. They have all the same benefits as traditional saunas, with the added comfort of lower room temperature. There are three kinds of infrared light: near infrared[NIR], mid infrared [MIR] and far infrared [FIR]. Far infrared is invisible to the naked eye and is referred to as infrared heat. Far infrared saunas work more directly. The water in your skin cells directly absorbs the radiation, converting it to heat. Your body gets hot and begins to sweat. When you enter an infrared sauna, the light permeates your skin, heating your cells from the inside .The Mayo Clinic reports that no adverse side effects have been reported with infrared saunas.

A 2015 study published in the Journal of American Medical Association found regular sauna visits can help people live longer because they reduce the

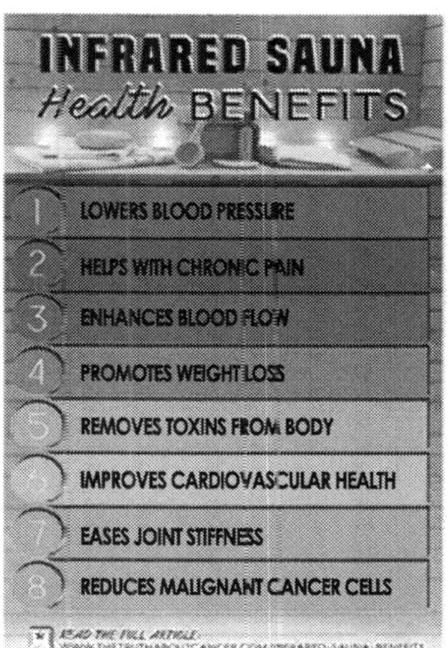

risk of certain cardiac problems. It lowers blood pressure, and helps with congestive heart failure because sitting in the sauna can raise heart rate and increase the calories they burn, giving their bodies the benefits of a workout even while sitting.

Infrared saunas have similar effects of mild exercise, and a healthy addition to your regular routine.

A study published in the Journal of Cancer Science and Therapy found that just after 30 days of infrared treatment, tumour infected mice saw reductions in their cancerous masses of up to 86%; even with low temperature infrared exposures of as little as 77 degrees Fahrenheit [25 Celsius]. In the blood, white cells, neutrophils,and lymphocytes become more active, which boosts biological defence mechanisms, giving the body the upper edge on fighting viruses and other infections. Saunas can increase the amount of antioxidants in one's body, which help repair and restore damaged cells. Infrared saunas affect all the systems in our body. The toxins in our body are typically stored in the upper layer of fat. Sweating can rid the body of these toxins from toxic drugs, pollutants, pesticides, and heavy metals, which in turn improves the immune system and overall health.

[https:www.healthyway.com/content/infrared-sauna-treatment]

EXERCISE Did you know gyms are the perfect hangouts for all sorts of germs ranging from norovirus to MRSA? These germs are hardy and can survive on gym surfaces for almost a month. Locker rooms are common places to find strep, fecal matter, and staph. The showers in the majority of gyms are filled with different bacteria like ringworm, warts, and athlete's foot bacteria. For someone who already has a suppressed immune system, it is highly recommended to stick to your disinfectant protocol: carry chemical free hand sanitizer and disinfectant wipes to protect your immune. Walking or running in a park connects you to nature and improves your mental as well as spiritual well-being.

We now have three generations of the CTV Williams and Mudryk 100 Km riding in support of donations for the Cross Cancer Institute.

A positive mindset that exercise and family support is tantamount to health and well-being, my 86-year-old father, Peter Szmyrko, rides his bike (which is older than he is) each year. My son Marty and grandsons Jesse and Teegan accompanied my dad Peter in this annual event every July. See details here: www.muddyphilanthropy.ca.

MASSAGE In 1886 Dr. William Murrell stated in the British Medical Journal, "Massage is of such inestimable value in the treatment of many intractable diseases, that it is regretted that, so little is known about it in this country, and that it is so rarely employed as a therapeutic agent." A growing body of evidence shows that massage therapy can be useful for a variety of health conditions: like releasing stress, reduces pain and anxiety, increases sleep and quality of life among cancer patients.

More information can be obtained on effective care for chronic pain by naturopath Case Adams, author of twenty-five books on natural healing.

REIKI Originated in Japan, it means universal life energy. The technique is based on the principal that the therapist can channel energy into the patient through light touch or hovering of the hands to activate the natural healing processes into the patient's body and restore physical and emotional well-being. It has been shown to help cancer patients, potentially treat complex regional pain syndrome Type 1 in children, aid in anxiety and depression for adults either in treatment or can be beneficial post-treatment. It is known to aid in dementia management, promote mental and physical well-being, can lower heart rate, blood pressure as well as increased immune strength.

One of the most stressful symptoms in oncology patients is cancer- related fatigue. The intention of a study, published in the European Journal of Cancer Cure, was to evaluate intervention using natural methods to help manage fatigue and psychological stress in patients with cancer. The study reviewed physical exercise, healing touch, therapeutic massage, nursing interventions and health education methods of healing. Several therapies showed that they helped reduce fatigue and stress. As a natural cancer treatment, it helps promote positive thoughts regarding healing and reduces stresses cancer can cause. Choose a Reiki practitioner you're comfortable working with.

ACUPUNCTURE is used to treat many illnesses and ailments in cancer patients. It is used to control pain, and to relieve nausea, vomiting, fatigue, hot flashes, neuropathy, anxiety, depression, and sleeping problems.

There are more than 2,000 acupuncture points along the meridians that are used to unblock the flow of QI (2 forces, yin and yang) that help restore a balance of emotional, mental and spiritual health. The most reliable evidence shows acupuncture helps with side effects of chemo such as pain, fatigue, loss of appetite and shortness of breath. Some relief is felt from nerve damage caused by chemotherapy and dry mouth caused by radiation. Always consult with your health professionals and research what works for you.

RAINDROP THERAPY This therapy is a great technique that uses essential oils feathered onto the spinal column for immune system support. It invigorates the mind, balances body energy, shields pathogens, promotes respiratory benefits, helps balance and ground the body, helps with structural alignment, helps with blood circulation and fluid retention, and helps with muscular spasms, stressed muscles and fatigue.

I recommend this essential oil support once a week for preventive measures and the relief of chronic disease, especially cancer patients looking for support of their immune system.

BATHS IN ESSENTIAL OILS By adding essential oils to your bath, you not only breathe them in but they help to detox from chemical interferences and rejuvenate your body cells. Adding eight to ten drops of any of the suggested essential oils to 1/4 cup mix of Epsom and Himalayan salts can help with side effects of cancer treatments due to immunity-assisting properties, and detoxing the body from chemicals.

Frankincense helps areas of digestion, the immune system, oral health stress/anxiety and respiratory concerns.

Clary Sage is used as a painkiller, antiseptic, helps calm the nervous system, fights depression and insomnia, and stimulates hair growth. Sclareol, part of the genetic makeup of sage, has shown some positive anti-cancer effects. It may help induce cancer cell death through apoptosis (which causes the cancer cell to self-destruct and stop the spread of cancer).

Lavender is a natural antioxidant and is considered a super healer by boosting immunity, relieving pain and improving blood circulation. It provided healing properties, relief to muscle, joints, and backaches.

Citrus oils may prevent tumour growth by inhibiting beta-signalling pathways. For cancer patients, a unique component of citrus oils is D-limonene which is a confirmed cancer-fighting agent. Lemon helps boost your immune, can help with headaches and fever while handing your mood.

Lemongrass has an astringent feature that helps speed up blood clotting and prevents hair loss. It helps remove toxins from the body and helps clean kidneys. Promising research shows lemongrass has anticancer activity and causes a loss in tumour cell viability.

Myrrh should not be used in excess but blends well with frankincense and lavender. It wards off inflammation and protects the circulatory system from toxins, relieves mucus and phlegm, and protects the systems and organs of your body.

Peppermint and Spearmint Both of these make a great tea for overcoming nausea and vomiting in the unfortunate side effect of chemo.

Divination Oil

3 drops SANDALWOOD
3 drops LAVENDER
3 drops PATCHOULI
1/2 cup Epsom Salts

Blend oils and add to the salts,
let them sit for awhile to infuse.
Use before divinatory work or
for just relaxing and centering.

Inspiration Bath

4 drops BERGAMOT
2 drops LEMON BALM
2 drops GRAPEFRUIT
1/2 cup Epsom Salts

Inspires contentment,
sharpens concentration,
and promotes creativity.

Cold Care Oil

5 drops EUCALYPTUS
3 drops LAVENDER
2 drops PEPPERMINT
1/2 cup Epsom Salts

Use anytime you feel congested
and achy. You can also add the
oils to 1 oz. of Sweet Almond Oil
and massage into arms, chest,
neck and abdomen before
going to bed.

Women's Bath

2 drops CLARY SAGE
3 drops LAVENDER
2 drops CHAMOMILE
2 drops ROSE GERANIUM
1/2 cup Epsom Salts

Add oils to full tub of warm water
and soak until water is cool.

MEDITATION is a type of mind-body therapy, a practice of concentrating or focusing your attention to increase mental awareness and calm your mind and body.

One of the most essential parts of meditation is conscious breathing or being aware of the way you breathe. Meditation can help lower your blood pressure and reduce stress and anxiety. You should practice meditation once or twice a day for short periods of ten to fifteen minutes. You can focus on being thankful, reflect on a calming poem, a piece of artwork that you find inspiring, or stroll through a nature walk or marked trail designed for meditation.

Research studies suggest regular meditation can reduce chronic pain, anxiety, improve sleep patterns, improve immunity and improve mood and anxiety in cancer patients.

The Lord is my Rock, my fortress, my place of safety.
He is my God, the Rock I run to for protection.
- Psalms 18:2

YOGA with or without essential oils.

Yoga is a great tool to bring awareness and harmony in both the mind and body. Most sessions include breathing exercises, meditation, and poses that stretch and flex various muscle groups. The relaxation techniques incorporated in yoga can lessen chronic pain, headaches, carpal tunnel syndrome, lower blood pressure and reduce insomnia.

Other physical benefits of yoga include increased flexibility, increased muscle tone and strength, improved respiration, energy and vitality, maintain a balanced metabolism, can help with weight reduction, helps with cardio and circulatory health, and improved athletic performance.

Yoga's incorporation of meditation and breathing can help improve a person's mental well-being. Regular yoga practice creates mental clarity, calmness, increases body awareness, relieves chronic stress patterns, relaxes the mind, and sharpens concentration.

Yoga, with essential oils, allows for early preventive action which enhances mental and emotional wellness. Essential oils such as Sandalwood, used for strengthening, cantering and Patchouli for grounding. Frankincense helps oxygenate the pineal and pituitary glands and helps increase the immune system, while peppermint helps promote awareness and unobstructed breathing. Bergamot helps relieve anxiety, depression, stress, and tension; when increasingly integrated into the holistic management and treatment of chronic diseases, including cancer, respiratory conditions including asthma, even migraines and heart disease reduces.

Do your research, even though essential oils are commonly sold in health food stores and grocery stores, beware - only high-grade oils, containing no artificial ingredients or chemical residues, should be used topically, inhaled or ingested.

Incorporating Essential Oils Into Your Daily Yoga Practice

DID YOU KNOW? Using essential oils in practice can conjure up the beautiful memories and feelings that you experienced during your practice, adding to the beneficial effects of the oils themselves.

Scents can trigger memory, emotions almost instantaneously, due to the olfactory bulb having access to the amydala (which processes emotion) and the hippocampus (for associative learning).

Purify & Cleanse

Diffuse before a class to bring about an uplifting energy of freshness and calmness.

3 drops LEMON
3 drops LIME
3 drops GERANIUM
3 drops YLANG YLANG

Meditation (dhyana)

Diffuse or inhale to deepen and enhance your practice. The oils help in grounding and expanding the upper chakras.

4 drops LAVENDER
4 drops FRANKINCENSE
4 drops ORANGE

Breathing (pranayana)

Swipe on your wrists, shoulders, temples and chest to open airways and encourage oxygen flow to the brain. This also gives you a whiff of oils with every change in pose.

4 drops PEPPERMINT
3 drops EUCALYPTUS
3 drops MARJORAM
3 drops LAVENDER
Mix in a 10ml roller ball with carrier oil.

Exercise (asana)

Use a roll-on or massage oil to alleviate muscle tension and soreness. Peppermint can also be used to increase mental focus and clarity.

4 drops WINTERGREEN
4 drops JUNIPER
4 drops EUCALYPTUS
3 drops LEMONGRASS
Mix in a 10ml roller ball with carrier oil.

Cleaning Your Mat

Use a diluted mixture of any of your favourite oil to spritz on your mat after every practice. This ensures a germ-free, sweat-free, fresh smelling mat!

1/2 cup water
20 drops LEMON
pinch of sea salt

REFLEXOLOGY is one of the most popular types of complementary therapy in the United Kingdom amongst people with cancer. Although there is no evidence that reflexology can cure or prevent any kind of disease, including cancer, it is still a vital therapy to help with nausea, pain, and cope with stress and anxiety. Reflexology combined with essential oils, can help boost the immune system, reduce nerve tingling and numbness from cancer drugs (peripheral neuropathy).

This combined therapy can help fight off colds and bacterial infections, reduce sinus problems, reduce back pain, reduce digestive problems, help relieve leg pain, lifts emotional distress and gives patients a feeling of well-being.

BIO-FEEDBACK THERAPIES Bio-feedback is a technique used to train your mind to control the way your body works and can help you reduce the severity and occurrence of headaches, insomnia, chronic pain and has not been found to affect cancer cells. During bio-feedback, a person is monitored with electrodes that are connected to electronic equipment to measure breathing, perspiration, skin temperature, blood pressure, heartbeat, and brain activity. These results are displayed on a computer screen. As an addition to your cancer treatment, bio-feedback can be an enjoyable experience helping relieve stress, anxiety, reprogram your mind to release negative thoughts, inner anger, and release emotional trauma, helping the body heal.

OMT (OSTEOPATHIC MANIPULATIVE THERAPY) is a manual therapy that treats problems by massaging or moving the relevant parts of the body, that includes massage, stretching muscles, tendons and ligaments, moving joints rhythmically, and muscle manipulation. Many cancer patients find that using this therapy helps them relax, helps control pain and tension and improves the overall feeling of health and well-being. Treatment sessions last thirty to forty-five minutes and three to six sessions are recommended to get the most benefits. Most evidence for osteopathy in cancer is based on reports by patients, osteopaths, and doctors saying it has helped. As always, consult with your health practitioners and research what works best for you.

VITAMINS and MINERALS There are lots of controversies whether to take vitamins and supplements while doing treatment. I speak from our own family experience having battled cancer three times, three different cancers, and receiving therapy. Western medicine and functional health science are not always on the same page, so you are best to research what works for you. The majority of oncologists are relatively strict in saying you should not be taking supplements during active treatments. However, as in our case, many patients do extensive reading online and research holistic studies about supplements and learn more about supplements than their oncologists do, which do not get much attention during their medical training.

We found taking supplements, as many as eighty per day, and ingesting essential oils as much as twenty-six bottles of 15 ml's per month, is a considerable support to helping curb side effects, especially through treatment. Supplements help support all cell structure and help to retain energy levels and better overall health. Using a combination of all the therapies is extremely useful for pro-active measures for overall better health, and emotional well-being. Studies have found that people who have higher levels of Vitamin D have significantly lower rates of breast, ovarian, renal, colon, pancreatic, aggressive prostate and other cancers. Some research indicates that B vitamins including folic acid can lower risk for some cancers, but large clinical trials have not been done to be conclusive.

Pharmaceutical and natural health products vary significantly in pro and con end results.

Personally, I have been doing a preventive intake of approximately thirty vitamins a day for about twenty years. I have stopped for a week or two when I have forgotten to take them on a road trip, and I can assure you my body complains in a few days, my energy levels drop, and my brain fog seems to return.

Always research your vitamin sources as not all are of good quality; get tested by a natural health practitioner that has access to full laboratories and use vitamins according to recommended dosages. Like fuel to your car, we need to top our systems up if they are to run smoothly. Today our foods are much too adulterated and chemically induced to give us the nutrition we need to stay healthy and focused.

Basic Essential Vitamin Guide

Research shows that two main reasons for taking vitamins are for overall health and wellness, and to fill in nutrient gaps. Science still demonstrates that multivitamins work for these purposes and provide enough reason for people to supplement their diets with some basic protocol. Men and woman are both as susceptible in experiencing low vitamin and mineral deficiencies with the higher probability for those who eat lots of takeout foods, packaged foods, or processed foods, as opposed to starting from scratch with home-cooked meals. Vegetarians and vegans are more likely to be low in vitamin B12, certain amino acids and omega-3, which is sourced from fish, seafood and meats.

On a global scale, soil depletion has resulted in crops being lower in nutrients than in past generations. A team of researchers at Austin's Department of Chemistry and Biochemistry studied agricultural data from 1950 to 1999 on forty-three different vegetables and fruits, finding reliable declines in the number of proteins, calcium, phosphorous, iron, vitamin B2, and vitamin C. Efforts to grow faster-growing varieties, pest resistant, bigger crops, and not working crop rotation, using more pesticides and herbicides all contribute to the decline of nutrients in our foods. A *Kushi Institute* analysis of nutrient data from 1975 to 1997 found that average calcium levels in twelve fresh vegetables dropped 27%, iron levels dropped 37%, vitamin A levels dropped 21%, and vitamin C levels dropped 30%.

Other studies published in the British Food Journal concluded that we would have to eat eight oranges to get the same amount of vitamin A our grandparents would have obtained from one.

Leaky gut issues can affect and interfere with how vitamins are absorbed daily. This is especially common in inflammatory bowel diseases, food allergy issues and digestive malfunctions. Many pharmaceutical drugs commonly block absorption of essential minerals and vitamins, especially cholesterol-lowering medicines, high blood pressure drugs and those used for diabetes that alter the natural pH environment of the upper GI tract. Heartburn medications can change vitamin D and B12 in our diets. If you rarely eat seafood, meat, eggs, or dairy, have a history of intestinal problems, take medications, eat lots of processed, refined or packaged foods, or have any chronic illness, then you probably have some shortfalls in vitamin deficiency.

In an ideal world, we would all eat organic, grass-fed, low-processed, garden fresh, locally grown, market vegetables and have healthier gut floral, with immune support and nutrient adequate diets; unfortunately, it is a fast-paced pre-packaged world that needs supplement supported foods. Estimates show that 75% of women would likely develop nutrient deficiencies if supplemental multivitamins did not exist.

Important Vitamin Supplements:

Vitamin D - is one of the most common deficiencies in both men and woman and is needed for maintaining strong bones, protect brain health, prevent mood disorders, help control cholesterol and blood pressure levels, and is capable of lowering inflammation.

Vitamin C - improves immunity against colds and infections, protects your vision and skin from free radicals like UV light and environmental pollution. It helps protect skin from aging and reduces skin cancer. Vitamin C is important for deterring age-related muscular degeneration and cataracts in older men and woman.

B Vitamins - Medications like acid-blocking drugs and those used to manage blood pressure or diabetes, can interfere with how vitamin B12 is metabolized in the body, and can lead to fatigue and central nervous system problems. A report from Harvard Medical School estimates 3-4% of all adults are severely low in B12.

B vitamins are also essential for metabolism, preventing fatigue, helps in developing fetuses and preventing congenital disabilities since it helps build the baby's brain and spinal cord. They can help with cellular processes, growth, and energy expenditure because they work with other vitamins like iron to make red blood cells and help turn calories into useable fuel (helpful for digestion). B's are essential for a menopausal woman to help support the nervous and hormonal systems.

Omega-3 - found in organic grass-fed animals, wild salmon, halibut, tuna, and important in preventing conditions like arthritis, heart disease, Alzheimer's, depression and inflammation. Extremely important for brain, heart and immune.

Our Western diet consists of plenty of omega-6 fatty acids, which are pro-inflammatory and found in many packaged foods and refined vegetable oils, but not enough omega-3 which are anti-inflammatory. Omega-3 fatty acids are the good types of fat and you have to eat them or take supplements as the body does not make them. They help your heart by curbing inflammation in blood vessels and in high doses, make abnormal heart rhythms less likely, lower your level of blood fats called triglycerides, and slow plaque buildup inside blood vessels.

You can also bring down your "bad cholesterol" by exercising, drinking less alcohol, and

cutting back on sugars and processed carbs like white bread and white rice. Some studies suggest omega-3 supplements may ease symptoms of ADHD. They are very important to brain development and brain function.

Calcium - Important for bone strength, crucial for regulating heart rhythms, aiding in muscle functions, controlling blood pressure and cholesterol levels, plus many other functions related to nerve signalling.

Multi-Vitamins - are a combination of different vitamins and help bridge nutrient gaps in your diet. WebMD Research shows men were 8% less likely to get cancer, lowered the risk of developing cataracts by 9%, keeps you energetic, has positive effects on a person's mood and emotional well-being and improves brain functions.

A recent study from Australia showed that B vitamins have a significant impact in supporting short-term memory function. The robust levels of minerals, antioxidants and B-complex vitamins help clear toxins from the body, facilitate enzymatic reactions required for detoxification, and keep the liver and other organs pristine. Numerous studies, particularly one with at least 1000mg of calcium and 1000IU of vitamin D can improve balance and risk of falls. Other studies have found correlations between hearing loss and vitamin-B complex. People with asthma and those prone to allergies often have depleted levels of vitamin C, zinc, selenium, and magnesium. Zinc is a requisite for testosterone production, the hormone of desire in both men and women, yet another reason why a potent daily multivitamin can boost libido and performance.

Supplement Safety - Look for evidence that shows how well the product works in scientific studies from credible publications. Always check the expiry date as some vitamins do expire. Be sure you research the brand you buy and that the source is viable. If you are on medications, talk to your doctor.

Vitamins A, D, E, and K can build up in your body so be sure to use recommended doses. If in doubt, always consult with your health professional.

More About Vitamins: Ningxia Wolfberry

World's most powerful antioxidant is making a huge impact for patients battling cancer, it made such a huge difference in my son's battle with cholangiocarcinoma. With this very rare and aggressive cancer of the bile ducts to the liver, he was given 3 months to live. NINGXIA wolfberry drink, Supplements, essential oils, and holistic functional science medicine gave him an extra 16 months.

The bile ducts are branched tubes that connect the liver and gallbladder to the small intestine. This cancer is not usually diagnosed until it has already spread beyond the ducts to the other tissues. The most common symptoms are jaundice, yellowing of the eyes, itching of the skin, dark coloured urine, which were Marty's initial symptoms. Our battle was huge and we needed everything we could get, to give him more months when the western world gave up on him.

He drank between 6-10 oz. of it daily to help his energy levels; it kept his immune system from crumbling, it kept his hemoglobin at normal levels in spite of chemo that did not work, and a trial that threw devastating blows to his body. Even when the cancer took its toll, 16 months after his given time was up, the doctor and nurses were totally amazed at his perfect blood work that remained that way till short of his passing. It was easy to drink and in spite of lack of appetite, and extreme weight loss he had good color throughout the 19 months of battle, his energy levels were surprisingly good. He was mobile and able to get out of bed, to the evening of his passing. As a mom, watching her son battle for his life, I could not believe the power behind this known wolfberry antioxidant liver protectant.

The Chinese WOLFBERRY has come to the modern world, mainly from the Yellow River in the NINGXIA region of China. In the mid 1980's when biochemists at NINGXIA Institute of Nutrition analyzed the NINGXIA wolfberry, they found that it is 15.6 percent protein, contain at least 21 essential minerals, and significant amounts of Vitamin B1, niacin (vitamin B3) and Vitamin C. It is the richest known whole food sources of Vitamin B1 or thiamin, which is essential for proper energy production, carbohydrate metabolism, and thyroid function.

It contains as much protein as raw oats, and is one of the richest known sources of plant protein. Protein is the building block of white blood cells and antibodies, which are part of the immune system that helps fight infection and defend the body against other foreign materials. They originate in the bone marrow, but circulate throughout the bloodstream.

The location where the NINGXIA wolfberry crop is grown is huge, all in the Yellow River flood Plain, where it derives its water from the foothills of the Bayan Har Mountains of the Himalayan range in Qinghai Provence in Northern China. As this water flows down through the mountain gorges, it becomes charged with super minerals and ends up in a silt-rich concentration that actually is yellow, thus the river named after.

Vitamins and minerals are key to longevity, and the NINGXIA wolfberry contains many of these vitamin-mineral pairs. Minerals are critical in body performances, such as electrolyte balance of our cells, nerve conduction for muscle contraction, bone and teeth formation, and enzyme activation. NINGXIA wolfberry is one of the highest whole food sources of potassium, which helps in neuron function of the brain and nerve, influencing osmotic balance between cells.

Zinc is critical for healthy immunity and the NINXGIA wolfberry has 5 times more zinc than the equivalent of brussels sprouts. It plays an essential role in the production of killer cells, gamma interferon and tumour necrosis factor alfa (is a cell signalling protein involved in systematic inflammation and is one of the cytokines that make up the acute phase reaction). If your system gets flooded with inflammation, in immune diseases like rheumatoid arthritis which often means you have too much tumour necrosis factor. (Doctors often refer to as TNF) The TNF is the signal that tells the rest of the defense units where to go and what to do. There is also a link between TNF and insulin resistance, a factor that leads to type 2 diabetes, so having the right amount of TNF is really important, otherwise can lead to inflammation and painful symptoms like psoriasis, joint swelling, bursitis, gout, and osteoporosis. According to research documented in ncbi.nlm.nih.gov suggests zinc can assist in reducing these systematic markers in many types of chronic inflammation. Clinical trial data supporting the value of zinc in reducing the duration and severity of the common cold when administered within 24 hours of the onset of cold symptoms is backed by Hulisz in the Journal of American Pharmaceutical Association.

NINGXIA wolfberry with 21 percent fibre by weight has got more fibre than bran and double the fibre of buckwheat. This makes it highly effective in removing triglycerides and cholesterol from the blood and lowering the risk of heart disease. Numerous studies have linked high intake of solvable fibre with lowered blood pressure and improved cardiovascular health. A high diet fibre has been directly linked to a lower risk of cancer, increased stability of blood sugars and lowered risk of heart disease.

The minerals, vitamins, phytonutrients and amino acids in NINGXIA wolfberry have been shown to protect the liver, eyes, heart, and cellular DNA from constant attack from free radicals and toxins. In 1998 Korean researchers discovered special compounds in these berries that afford powerful protection for the most important organ in the body, being the liver. Known as pyrroles and cerobrosides, these nutrients have shown to protect damage to the liver caused both by toxins and hepatitis. During 15 years of studies, documentation shows NINGXIA wolfberries to be cardioprotective, anticancerous, and immune stimulating. The polysaccharices in NINGXIA wolfberry positively affect natural killer cell function, which help fight cancer.

In 2003, the Institute of Medicinal Biotechnology study at the Peking Union Mecical College in Beijing, China, found that NINGXIA wolfberry polysaccharides stimulated production of interleukin-2, a non inflammatory part of immunity that protects against cancer cells and microbial invasion. A 2004 study at Huazhong University of Science and Technology, found that polysaccharide-fed animals could also resist the growth of transplanted cancer tumour cells (sarcoma S180).

In 1994, Tufts University developed a powerful new method of assaying the antioxidant capacity of common foods called Oxygen Radical Absorbance Capacity (ORAC). The ORAC is currently the most reliable method for calculating a food's antioxidant potential against a free radical peroxyl, which is the second most common radical in the human body. The ORAC of NINGXIA wolfberries data published to date is the highest known score of any food in the world, with 5 times the antioxidant capacity of prunes, 10 times that of oranges, 12 times of raisins, and 55 times that of cauliflower.

Gerontologists at the department of Cell Biology and Genetics at Peking University discovered that including small amounts of NINGXIA wolfberry in the culture, could extend the number of times human lung cells could divide from 49 to 61 times. Each time a cell divides, the chance of error creeps in, as well as free radical damage. Using the wolfberry nutrient, researchers effectively increased the life span of the lung tissue by 22 percent.

During the past two decades, a number of clinical trials have shown a direct link between cancer, accelerated aging, and poor immune function. Research at the Mount Sinai Medical Centre in New York showed a link between low immunity and poor outcomes in cancer survival.

NINGXIA WOLFBERRY, the highest antioxidant food known, makes it an excellent whole food choice with 18 amino acids, 21 trace minerals, Vitamin B1-B2-B6-C and E, polyphenols, carotenoids, magnesium and potassium.

I personally saw amazing results that my son had in his battle, results that gave him quality of life by drinking the NINGXIA wolfberry every single day. Nothing else could have or would have sustained him in that way. I take 2-6 oz. of the NINGXIA wolfberry everyday too. For me, it's about being proactive!!

Turkish Pilaf with Wolfberries Recipe

2 large garlic cloves
85 grams organic brown rice
3 celery sticks, finely chopped
1 medium onion, halved and very thinly sliced
1 generous pinch of saffron
1/2 tsp ground cinnamon
1 Tbsp fresh thyme leaves
100 grams baby spinach leaves
3 tsp coconut oil
1 tsp vegetable bouillon
1 Tbsp dried wolfberries
25 grams flaked almonds
200 grams turkey thigh, diced

Finely chop the garlic and set aside. Meanwhile, pour 2 Tbsp of boiling water over the saffron and set aside to infuse. Heat 2 tsp of cocnut oil in a large saute pan with a lic, then add the diced turkey and fry for 5 minutes, stirring frequently until it starts to brown.

Stir the rice and cinnamon into the pan, then pour in 400 millilitres of boiling water and the bouillon, and stir well. Add the celery, thyme, wolfberries and lots of ground black pepper. Cover the pan tightly to prevent steam escaping, and cook over low heat for 20 minutes.

Meanwhile, heat the remaining oil in a pan and add the onion. When it starts to soften, cover the pan for 5 minutes to steam it a little more. Take off the lid and slowly fry for 12 to 15 minutes until golden, stirring frequently.

After the rice has cooked for 20 minutes, check the water level -- if the rice is still too nutty and the liquid has all been absorbed, add up to 100 millilitres more water. Stir in the saffron, cover again and cook for 5 to 10 minutes until the rice is tender.

Add the garlic and spinach, cook briefly to wilt the leaves, and then turn off the heat. Toss through the fried onions and almonds, and serve.

Check the Advertisements page for more information on
our journey with Ningxia Wolfberry products.

Frozen Ningxia Popsicles Recipe

Try either of these delicious Ningxia-Wolfberry recipes
for healthy, chemical-free treats!

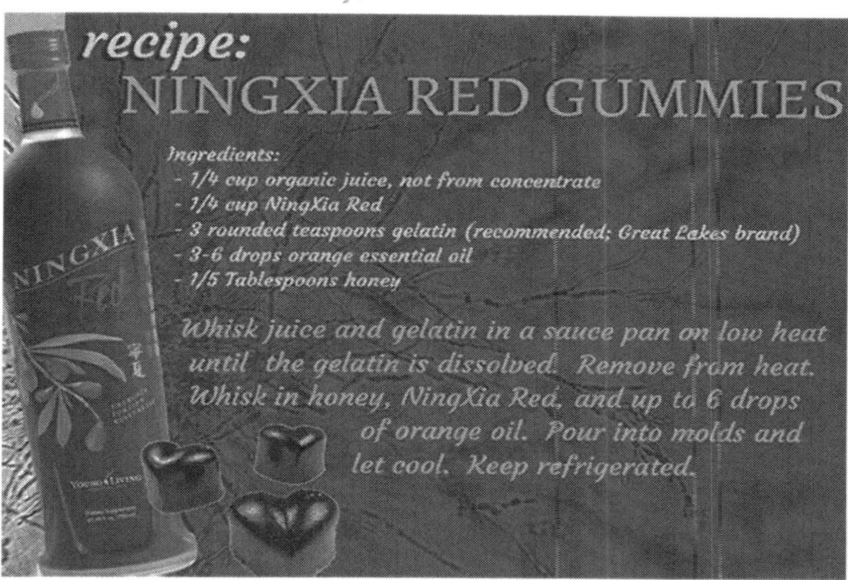

Chapter 10:

Herbs and Essential Oils
Let's talk "Simple Solutions, Healthy Choices"

My Great Grandmother on my dad's side was an herbalist in Europe. Although I never got to meet her, I became very intrigued with herbs and oils when my youngest son was diagnosed with cancer. Many times I wished I had met her and could learn from her, but her spirit lives in me because so much of my knowledge comes as easily as the magic in those herbs. I remember my Grandmother picking different plants in the forest and the garden and either drying them for internal use, boiling them for tinctures, or infusing them for balms. Back then it was critical for their survival.   There was dandelion root tincture for gout, eczema, acne and also was a great stimulant for liver disorders. Red Clover freshly chopped was used for insect and bee bites. Chickweed infused oil was used in bath water for eczema and skin rashes. One of my favourite things to do as a kid was picking pigweed; it certainly grew plentiful on the farm where we lived. I would add butter, garlic, onions and sautéed it like spinach. It had a mild flavour and would take on the stronger flavoured garlic and onions for a very yummy meal enriched in Vitamin C, A, iron and calcium. The leaves could also be used in salad.

Herbs over the centuries were classified as either stimulating or sedating, relaxing or astringent, and were used to achieve balance in both body tissues and the nervous system. For example irritable bowel syndrome, might be treated with chamomile to sedate the nervous system and relax the digestive tissues, followed by a stimulant such as ginger to encourage the vital force and internal energy levels. Both can be made into teas and drank daily. We are so fortunate today that many of the garden grown herbs are also available in high quality essential oils.

My personal experience with Young Living is so exciting because they have over 40 essential oils approved by Health Canada as flavourings. For example - Basil, Oregano, Dill, Cumin, Black Pepper, Cinnamon Bark, Rosemary, Parsley and lots of citruses such as Lemon, Lime, Orange and Lemongrass. Cooking with essential oils and sprinkling with herbs has given a whole new life to the meaning of delicious.

> " From food are
> born all creatures,
> which live upon food
> and after death,
> return to food "

My Favourite DIY...   **'Sweet & Tangy Balsamic Vinaigrette Recipe'**

2 tsp each of honey, balsamic vinegar and Dijon mustard
4 drops either Lime+, Lemon+ or Orange+ EO food flavouring
4 Tbsp organic extra virgin olive oil

Whisk all ingredients together till combined.
Pairs well with fresh basil, roma tomatoes and mozzarella balls.

FOOD is chief of all things. It is therefore said to be "medicine of all diseases of the body" as quoted from The Upanishads, 500 B.C.

Herbs in the garden offer a rewarding combination of beauty and usefulness; they can be tucked into existing flower beds or vegetable beds. They are adaptable and can grow in patio pots on the balcony or indoors. Wherever you decide to plant them they cultivate peace and enchantment and can become your special Zen area.

There are several types of herb gardens. One of my favourite is the "AROMATIC HERB GARDEN", where you find a variety of softly-scented herbaceous plants including winners such as Rosemary, Sage, Thyme, Lemon Verbena, Lavender, Orange Mint and Lemon Balm.

My second favourite is the "CULINARY HERB GARDEN" which you want immediate access to for everyday cooking. Its here you will find lettuce, leeks, dill, coriander, arugula, calendula, chives and parsley. If you are a salad lover you should plant each herb one foot square or a row four feet long for your salad greens in a sunny, wind protected area. I absolutely love my raised cedar bed four feet by twelve feet.

There are many other themed herb gardens, such as "MEDICINAL HERB" gardening. It must be recognized that plants are potent drugs. Their active ingredients, isolated can be as potent as aspirin (wintergreen and birch essential oils) some can trigger allergic reactions to susceptible people and of course some plants can be toxic and lethal. That being said, most herbal remedies are safe and boast that many common ailments can be treated at home. I always maintain that you can stay healthy by including herbs and essential oils in your daily diet.

In years past, I can remember my mother giving all six of us, that dreaded Cod liver oil and bitters. Herbal tonics in the past were taken in spring especially to restore the body's vitality after a winter diet lacking in fresh vegetables. Yarrow, dandelion, sage, peppermint, and rose hip tonic helped to cleanse the system and strengthen the whole body. These herbs are all considered medicinal.

Of course never try an herbal remedy as a substitute for medical attention or if you are pregnant. If a minor disorder continues to persist, it should be diagnosed and treated by a medical professional. Never take herbs or essential oils in excess, or if you are uncertain about a plant, be sure to connect with a herbalist or aromatherapist for professional advice.

The Right Way to Gather, Store, and Prepare Herbs

Let's talk a bit about practical information on cultivation, harvesting and preserving herbs. We have discussed garden herbs, so let's explore what Mother Nature has to offer in the wild.

Gathering should be undertaken at the right time. For flowers, pick at the beginning of flowering. For leaves, before or during flowering. Roots should be dug out in early spring or fall, and berries picked at the time of ripening. Gather on sunny days in dry conditions. Extra moisture can present a mould issue in the infusion of tinctures.

Pick only healthy clean plants that are free from pests, herbicides and pesticides. Stay away from railroad tracks, ditches industrial areas and contaminated water areas.

Always take ten percent of the crop, leaving plenty for next year's growth. Do not crush the flowers or leaves while drying and do not use plastic bags or containers. The herbs begin to sweat and later turn black upon drying. Do not wash the herbs before drying. Spread them thinly on a dryer screen, or cotton cloth. Do not put them in direct sun to dry but keep them in a well ventilated area. If you dry them in the oven keep the heat at 35 degrees Celsius or 95 degrees Fahrenheit.

Keep dried herbs in glass jars in a cool dark place for no longer than one season as they lose healing power. Every year should be a new season of harvest.

Making Herbal Remedies

For thousands of years, plants have been used for the benefit of mankind in treatment of many diseases. In recent years, plant remedies have been neglected by orthodox medicine in favour of synthetic drugs, not always to the benefit of the patient; however, there is a huge revival of interest in back-to-nature remedies my grandmothers used that worked and caused fewer side effects.

Some of you might have heard or used some of these hand-me-down remedies tried and tested on my own family that are simple, effective and in some cases infused with essential oils to enhance the healing properties.

This is the exciting part of herbs, so let's chat about several ways you can use them to your benefit. The following methods are those I have tried and love. Keeping it simple is best. Be sure your herbs are properly dried for a few days, so very little moisture is retained. This insures your infusions do not take on mould and spoil.

Infused oils will last up to a year if kept in a cool dark place, although smaller amounts made fresh are more potent. My rule of thumb is use within six months for best results, regardless if you use herbs or essential oils in your herbology mix unless you can store them in the refrigerator, it can extend the time frame to one year. Honestly, mine are used up well before the expiry.

Hot Infusion

Pack a mason jar tightly with your herb of choice and cover it completely with oil. My favourite oils are organic olive oil, sunflower oil, almond or camellia oil. All of these oils have good therapeutic effects on your skin. [see more on carrier oils on page 31] Cover with the lid and place the jar in a slow cooker on high. Add boiling water so its half way up the jar. Place a foil wrap over the jar and the cooker so the heat stays inside. I actually bring the infusion to a gentle boil and then turn it to low for 3-4 hours. I then let it cool and stand for a couple days. Depending on the herb, the oil will take on the infusion aroma and I must say Black Spruce is my favourite. Pour the mixture in a sieve, use a cheese cloth or wine press to extract the oil from the pulp. At this time I will infuse with essential oils. Pour into clean airtight storage jars and keep in a cool dark place until you are ready to make ointments, creams, massage oil or salves.

Pack the jars tight with dandelion heads. Fill to cover with organic oil of choice. Place jar in crock pot and simmer on low for 3-4 hours. Remove the jar from the crock pot and leave it to set for several days before straining the pulp from the unfusion.

Cold Infusion

Very similar to hot infusion, pack the jar tightly, pour oil over the herb until it is completely covered. Put the lid on and leave the jar in a warm area of your house or a greenhouse, but preferably out of direct sunlight. Sunlight can decrease the potency of the healing properties. Rotate the jar every other day taking out any air bubbles that accumulate. It should be ready in 2-3 weeks depending on the aroma you want to achieve. The longer it stands the stronger the aroma. Extract the oil in the same methods as hot infusion. Some prefer to pack fresh herbs in the once-infused oil and repeat the process. Strain again and store in clean glass jars in a cool dark place. I like to refrigerate mine until I need to use them. Pure organic olive oil will solidify. Cold infusion is successful only if herbs are dried, otherwise mould will appear in a few days.

Making Tea Infusions

Use herbs in the same way you would use loose tea. The water should be just off the boil since vigorously boiling water disperses valuable volatile oils in the steam. Use this method for flowers and leafy parts of the plant. You can use dried or fresh herbs, or essential oils of the same plant. Generally use one tablespoon of herbs to a 6 oz. teacup. Pour over the water and let it steep for 10 minutes. Some like to strain the herbs but often I will eat them once I finished my tea. If you are using essential oils approved for flavouring you only need a drop. Good quality of Lemon essential oil has the potency of 17 lemons. Because its oil is taken from the rind it is very smooth tasting and has no acidic or bitter aftertaste. You can make three or four cups at a time and drink it hot or cold. Always make fresh for the day. Use any dries herbs used as peppermint, Moringa tree leaves, yarrow, nettle, cinnamon bark, marigold, rosemary, sage, lavender or a mix of any of your favourites.

Decoctions

This is a more vigorous extraction of plants' active ingredients. You can use the roots, bark, twigs, berries, flowers, or a combination. In a pot, add the herbs, pour over cold water and simmer on low for a couple hours. Make it fresh everyday and drink it hot or cold.

Powders and Capsules

These are always fun to do. You can purchase ready to assemble capsules online. Be sure to order size 00 because I find them easiest to swallow and they hold 200-250 mg of powdered herb. Recommended dose is 2-3 capsules daily. The kit has all the tools necessary to fill and complete each capsule. Always purchase gelatin or vegetarian capsules organic if possible. You can also mix 4-6 drops flavouring approved essential oils in the capsules. I like these especially at cold flu season. Essential oils like oregano, cinnamon bark, lemon, frankincense amongst others can be dropped into the capsules and froze. The oils will eat through the capsule and leak out after several weeks, so best to do a 2 week supply up at a time.

Compress

I still remember my grandmother using compresses often for sore muscles, bites, infections and sunburn. Take a clean terry cotton cloth or gauze and soak it in the heated herbal infusion. Once saturated, squeeze it out and apply to the area. When it cools, repeat the process if necessary. Peppermint and black spruce compresses are great for headaches too. Use an herb-infused compress with essential oils for maximum results.

Poultice

This was another of my grandmother's favourite. Poultice is similar to a compress except the whole herb was applied verses soaking the gauze in the extract. She would pick the cold leaves and apply to the affected area, then tie it with gauze to hold the herb in place. This could stay for hours or overnight. You can also chop up the herbs, boil them for 2 minutes, cool to warm temperature and apply directly to the area. Hold it in place by wrapping it with gauze and leave it in place overnight if needed.

Wild Comfrey

Wild Strawberry

Wild Dogwood

Steam Inhalants

One of the easiest and most effective ways to support respiratory issues is with steam inhalation. Using herbs or essential oils for conditions such as mucus, asthma, sinusitis, COPD and lung cancer can help bring relief. Place 2 tablespoons dried herbs in a bowl. Peppermint, oregano, lemon, wintergreen works well. Pour boiling water over it. Lean over the bowl with a towel draped over the bowl, and inhale for as long as you can bear the heat or until the mixture cools. You can add essential oil drops to enhance the experience. Diffusing essential oils complements this procedure and doubles its effectiveness. Always use good quality organic essential oils and herbs. Adding several diffusers with 10-12 drops of essential oils to your living areas have profound effects on all your energy centers. Essential oils can continue to stimulate in real time, and gently continue respiratory support long after the steam application has stopped working. Herbs and essential oils are hand in glove therapy and I love that both have calming and therapeutic properties for a general overal feeling of well-being.

Add a diffuser year-round to the Zen area of your home. It's especialy comforting during cold, dreary winter months.

I certainly encourage you to connect with Mother Earth and a l her goodness. n many parts of the world, herbs are the only option for all types of health problems. We have such an amazing resource at our disposal - herbs and essential oils are a definite alternative to the over the counter drugs.

Herbs in the kitchen cupboard such as garlic, ginger and herbal teas provide some of the most useful first aid remedies. For example:

You can rub garlic on acne and other infected pimples to draw out infection.

Place a fresh slice of onion on an insect sting for rapid relief. It's also used to relieve nettle rash or hives caused by food allergens.

Keep an assortment of dried herbs or herbal tea bags handy for herbal infusions. Drinking chamomile tea can be helpful for shock and nervous upsets, and a cup in the evening before going to bed encourages a restful sleep.

Apply aloe vera gel from the split leaf directly to burns, wounds, dry skin, fungal infections, and insect bites. You can also use several leaves split in half to collect a large quantity of gel. Boil it down to a thick paste and store the paste in clean glass jars in a cool place.

Most home remedies are quite safe, but they should be treated with respect. Do not exceed the stated doses or continue with home remedies if conditions are persistent or worsening or if a true diagnosis is in doubt. Home remedies or herbalism has always been regarded as the "medicine of the people" – simple remedies that can be used at home for minor minor illness or to supplement more potent remedies prescribed by professionals for chronic and acute conditions.

This chapter gives you just a small overview of the hundreds of different recipes and the enormous potential of the versatile and rewarding herbs and plants that are at your disposal. There are many books that you can tap into, either online or at your favourite library. Get creative, build an herb garden, take a walk with Mother Nature, or invest in some trusted organic teas. Whatever you enjoy, herbs and essential oils can expand your experience to new wellness.

The journey is truly amazing.

Herb drying tables can be built large or small depending on your individual needs. I love my layered drying table that can accommodate many different herbs at once.

Chapter 11

Terry's Timeless Recipes
Blended in "**God's Pharmacy**"

My absolute favourite thing to do is mix essential oils, infuse herbs, dry leaves for herbal tea, and experiment with natural ingredients that make powerful tools for many ailments, support the immune system, and help improve overall health.

The following pages have recipes that I have personally blended and tried on myself, family, friends and clients. Natural Healing has been around from the beginning of time, long before western medicine and big pharma was established. I love the effects and medical properties of plants, the lifeline of a plant extracted or distilled, to become an essential oil. Mixing herbs that have been either hot or cold compressed with essential oils is life's natural remedies which God in His Greatness has provided. I am so blessed to be able to share with you some recipes that are chemical free and can help support your wellness without fear of side effects western medicine offers.

I am aware that mainstream medicine and most health professionals may scoff at these less scientific yet hard-to-dismiss empirical treatments. May this collection of formulas and recipes let you decide for yourself. In our journey we had no choice, but to find solutions and protocols when western medicine failed us; to research more, blaze a trail of unknowns, and find balance between healthier options and pharmaceuticals. The fact my son lived 13 months longer than any oncologist was willing to give him, gives me peace at heart knowing there is merit to treating the disease rather than the effects.

Although the therapeutic effects of many herbs and essential oils have not been scientifically proven, much research in the last five years continues to identify the active ingredients that one day will be the basis of medicine that will destroy cancer cells and other chronic illnesses. Much has already been discovered.

Removing chemicals and synthetics from our medicine by using herbal remedies designed to help the body heal by itself has been encouraged by the Chinese who work with about 5800 known herbs and extracts. The Greeks in the first century boasted 400 herbs and in India 2500, with at least 800 regularly collected from the tropical rainforests of Africa, and almost 300 detailed for the medical profession in Germany. Many thousands more are known to healers around the world including our North American Natives who encourage Sweat houses, herbalism and spiritual energies. Despite the huge array of healing plants, western herbalists have working knowledge of about 200 plants. Herbs and essential oils of high quality grade with no adulterated process, no herbicides and pesticides can be your everyday cooking, bathing, massaging and inhaling remedies so good for you.

It is my hope that this book can encourage you to once again take responsibility for your own health. May this be your starting point of lifestyle change. But as always, if you are unsure, consult a health care professional you can trust to have your best interests at heart.

Maintain balance in your life, get out in the fresh air, eat well, and experience all the healing herbs and plants Mother Nature has to offer. Meditate.

DISCLAIMER: Opinions expressed in this presentation are solely our team Oilers for Life and do not express the views or opinions of Young Living. Young Living does not endorse, is not responsible for, and makes no representations or warranties regarding such content or its accuracy. I encourage you to verify the explanations and opinions presented. Young Living shall not be liable for any harm resulting from or in connection with reliance on any such content. DO YOUR OWN RESEARCH!!!

Pain Be GONE

Day Use
I love this mix for any heavy pain! Use as often as the pain comes back... every hour, or whatever interval is needed. Works for my scoliosis and sciatica, plus any back or hip issues.

Night Use
Rub on the entire spine. Rub directly on the area of pain. Rub on the underside of your feet, from big toe to heel.

In 2 oz of Ortho Ease Massage Oil, mix the following:

30 drops Northern Lights Black Spruce
30 drops Deep Relief

30 drops Panaway	**15 drops Thyme**
20 drops Copaiba	**15 drops Rosemary**
20 drops Relieve It	**15 drops Basil**
15 drops Frankincense	**15 drops Aroma Siez**
15 drops Lavender	**10 drops of Peppermint**

Get your Sleep
Stop the Stress

In a 15ml roller ball or spray bottle, mix:

20 drops Frankincense
15 drops Lavender
12 drops Sandalwood
12 drops Vetiver
10 drops Copaiba
10 drops Marjoram
10 drops Valor
10 drops RC
10 drops Stress Away
5 drops Peace & Calming
5 drops Peppermint

Fill with carrier oil such as camelia, coconut, olive or avocado oil.

Sleep Better & Snore Less!

Excellent support for your nervous, respiratory, circulatory and cardiovascular systems!

For sleep before bed at night, apply to the back of the neck, behind the ears, and the bottoms of your feet. This is one powerhouse blend for sleep issues... I use it and love it!

For snoring, apply to the back of the neck and the throat areas, just before bed.

It's also great for stress - use every 3 hours for stress and anxiety by applying behind the ears and to the back of the neck.

Bathe at least 3 times a week in any of these oils (choose a combination of 10 drops total) along with 1/2 cup Epsom Salts. Change the oils up each bath. Soak for 20-30 minutes before bedtime.

Roller Bottle Recipes

***DIFFUSER ~ use the same essential oil combos for your Diffuser for added body system support**

Use 10 ml roller ball and carrier oil. Mix with YL V-6 Massage Oil, Sunflower Oil, or Safflower Oil. Be sure carrier oils are organic, cold press, and unrefined.

Exhaustion Blend #1
** to relax*
2 drops Bergamot
1 drop Clary Sage
2 drops Elemi
2 drops Frankincense
2 drops Lavender

Exhaustion Blend #2
** to increase energy*
2 drops En-R-Gee
2 drops Grapefruit
2 drops Rosemary
2 drops Lemon
2 drops Joy

Cold/Flu Season
3 drops Thieves
3 drops R.C.
4 drops Raven
2 drops Eucalyptus

Lift & Calm Blend
2 drops Sandalwood
1 drop Cypress
2 drops Ylang Ylang
2 drops Bergamot
2 drops Vetiver
1 drop Black Pepper

Mental Clarity Blend
2 drops Rosemary
1 drop Lemon
1 drop Cypress
4 drops Brain Power

Face Lotion
3 drops Frankincense
1 drop Purification
1 drop Lavender

Sleepy Blend
4 drops Lavender
2 drops Marjoram
4 drops Cedarwood
2 drops Clary Sage

Focus Formula
1 drop Frankincense
1 drop Vetiver
1 drop Cedarwood
1 drop Clarity
1 drop Lavender
3 drops Brain Power
1 drop Patchouli

Muscle/Joint Pain Rub
2 drops Deep Relief
1 drop Thyme
2 drops Wintergreen
2 drops Rosemary
4 drops PanAway
2 drops Copaiba
4 drops Northern Lights Black Spruce

ADHD Blend
5 drops Lavender
5 drops Cedarwood
5 drops Vetiver
5 drops Peace & Calming

Allergy Bomb
5 drops Lavender
5 drops Lemon
5 drops Peppermint

Healing Blend
4 drops Lavender
4 drops Melaleuca

Motivational Blend
1 drop Black Pepper
2 drops Lime
2 drops Orange
2 drops Frankincense

ESSENTIAL OILS SHOULD BE SAFELY ADMINISTERED ACCORDING TO DILUTION CHARTS AND INSTRUCTIONS. THESE STATEMENTS HAVE NOT BEEN EVALUATED BY THE FDA. THESE PRODUCTS ARE NOT INTENDED TO DIAGNOSE, TREAT, CURE, OR PREVENT ANY DISEASE.

Dry**Nose** *recipes*

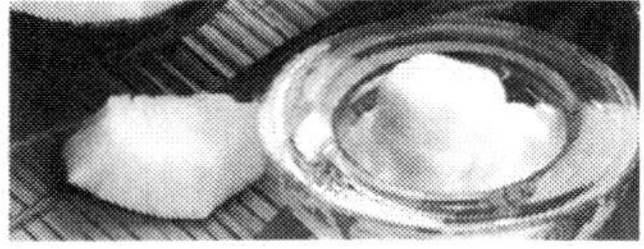

Recipe #1... COCONUT SALVE

1 teaspoon coconut oil *(warm it until semi-solid)*
8 drops German Chamomile *(regenerates skin, great for chapped lps & acne)*
5 drops Frankincense
2 drops Eucalyptus

Pour into small glass container.
Use a cotton swab to apply to the
inside of each nostril so there is a
good coating.
Apply 3 times a day and especially
before you go to bed.

*This essential oil blend works great to relieve
dryness, soreness, etc caused by dry winter air
or lack of mositure. Awesome all year long!*

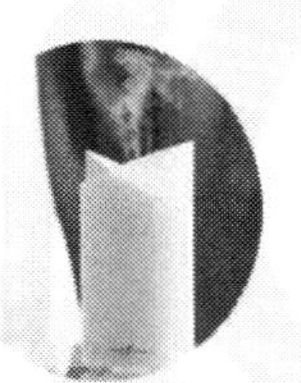

Recipe #2... DIFFUSER

For help this cold & flu season, diffuse 24/7
(always have your diffuser going) 10-12 drops
of any combination of the following oils:

**Thieves, R.C., Raven, Purification, Palo Santo,
Frankincense, Lavender, Lemon, Eucalyptus,
Tea Tree, Oregano.**

Recipe #3... STEAM BOWL

Create a Steam Bowl by boiling several
cups of water, and adding 2-3 drops of
any of the oils listed in Recipe #2 to the
hot water.
Drape a towel over your head to trap
the steam and inhale for 15 minutes.
You can also apply Coconut Salve
(Recipe #1) as directed.

Recipe #4... PEPPERMINT TEA

Put 1-2 drops of Peppermint Oil in hot
water for a wonderful peppermint tea.

Spray for
Sore Throat

In a small spray bottle, mix:

- **2 drops Peppermint**
- **2 drops Thieves**
- **2 drops Clove**
- **2 drops Lemon**
- **2 drops Oregano**
- **2 drops Melaleuca**

Add 1/4 teaspoon Himalayan salt crystals, fill with water and shake well. Use as often as needed. Also works well as a hand sanitizer!

Mr. Vic's Mix for
Stuffy Nose &
Nasal Congestion

In a 10ml roller ball, mix:

- **1 drop Peppermint**
- **2 drops Rosemary**
- **5 drops Tea Tree**
- **5 drops Eucalyptus**

Top up roller ball bottle with carrier oil. Mix well then apply on chest, spine & bottoms of feet for relief from congestion and other cold symptoms.

Essential Oil Diffuser Blend for
Cold Relief

- **2 drops Lemon**
- **2 drops Purification**
- **3 drops Frankincense**
- **3 drops Peppermint**
- **4 drops RC**

<u>Roller Ball option:</u>

In a 10ml roller ball, add the above essential oils and top up with a carrier oil like Ortho Ease massage oil, V-6 massage oil, camelia, jojoba, or olive oil. Mix well.

Apply to chest, spine & bottoms of feet 3 times daily for relief of nasal congestion or sinus infection. Great for keeping in your pocket!

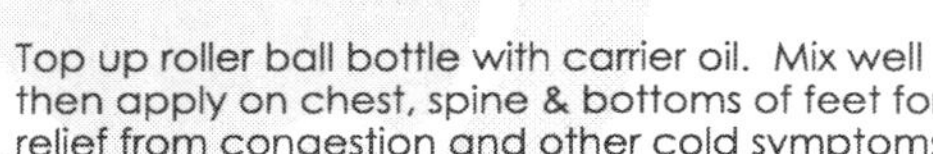

FIRST AID
ON THE GO ESSENTIALS *with young living essential oils*

Essential Oils can be used to treat minor First Aid incidents. Create your own First Aid Emergency Kit which can be used when camping, hiking, or traveling. Send it with your family when they go on outings. Keep it in your car for emergencies.

Use additional First Aid best practices when treating minor injuries. Remember to call 911 and consult with qualified professionals to treat sever injuries requiring First Aid. Essential Oils can be used to supplement qualified professional assistance and First Aid best practices, not replace them.

Mix a combination of any essential oils to a total of 30 drops per 10ml roler ball. Top with carrier oil.

Young Living has oils for First Aid...

ANTI-BACTERIAL: Clean wound with soap and water. Apply oils topically to disinfect a cut or wound.
Use any of the following oils topically. Dilute 4 drops carrier oil to 1 drop EO (4:1) Oregano, Thyme, Melaleuca, Clove, Cinnamon.

BONES: Apply oils topically to a bone bruise, fracture, or break. Mix more as needed.
Use any of the following oils topically. Dilute 2 drops carrier oil to 1 drop EO (2:1) Wintergreen, Deep Rel ef, Panaway, Relieve-It, Fir, Marjoram.

BRAIN: Apply oils topically to temples, back of the neck, or spine for a head or neck injury.
Use any of the following oils topically. Dilute as necessary. Frankincense, Cypress, Peppermint, Bergamot.

BRUISE: Apply oils topically to the bruised area.
Use any of the following oils topically. Dilute as necessary. Helichrysum, Geranium, Lavender, Panaway, Basil, Aroma Siez.

BURN: For minor First Degree burns, submerse the injured area in cool water. Apply oils topically to affected area.
Use any of the following oils topically. Dilute as necessary. Lavender, Melaleuca, Roman Chamomile, Peppermint.

CALM: To soothe anxious feelings or stress associated with an injury apply the oils topically to the temples or back of neck. Or place a few drops of oils to the palm of hands and breathe in.
Use any of the following: Peace & Calming, Orange, Vetiver, Lavender, Stress Away, Tranquil, Frankincense, Cedarwood.

CLEAN: To clean or disinfect hands, cuts and abrasions.
Use Tea Tree, Thieves, Purification, Lemon, Melaleuca, or Orange in your hands or on affected area. Dilute as necessary.

CRAMPS: To soothe cramping muscles or Charley Horses, apply a few drops to the affected area and gently massage.
Use Panaway, Lemongrass, Marjoram, Basil, Aroma Siez, Wintergreen, Valor, or Peppermint. For stomach cramps, use Digize.

CUT: To provide relief to a cut, scrape, or abrasion apply topically to the affected area.
Use Melaleuca, Lavender or Frankincense to support skin regeneration, and Helichrysum to help stop bleeding.

IMPORTANT NOTE: Always dilute Essential Oils (EO) with a Carrier Oil like Coconut Oil when applying. Use the Oil Dilution chart provided below. Never apply undiluted Essential Oils direct to an open wound, in your ears or near mucus membranes.

All Purpose
Bathroom Cleaner

Non-Toxic & Effective...
use on all surfaces!

8 oz Water in a spray bottle + **1 capful Thieves** + **10 drops each Lemon, Tea Tree & Purification** + **2 capfuls Vodka or White Rum**

Use on all areas of your home and office.
It's the only cleaner you really need!

Glass Cleaner

Ingredients:

**1 capful of Thieves Household Cleaner
5 drops of Lemon Essential Oil
1 tsp of white vinegar
3 cups of water**

Mix all ingredients together in a spray bottle.
Apply liberally to glass/mirror surfaces and wipe
dry with a lint-free cloth.

All-Natural DIY BUG & INSECT SPRAY REPELLENTS

In a 4 oz spray bottle, mix:
- **2 oz distilled water**
- **2 oz witch hazel**
- **5 drops Purification**
- **10 drops Thieves**
- **10 drops Peppermint**
- **15 drops Citronella**
- **20 drops Eucalyptus**

Spray mixture on skin to repel ants, mosquitos & other bugs.

CAUTION: AVOID SPRAYING NEAR EYES.
NOT RECOMMENDED FOR UNDER 6 YEARS OF AGE.
DILUTE MIXTURE WITH MORE WATER FOR
CHILDREN UNDER 6.

MOSQUITO SPRAY REPELLENTS

OPTION 1
EUCALYPTUS LEMON

In a BPA-free spray bottle, mix:

4 oz distilled water

5 drops lemon essential oil

10 drops eucalyptus essential oil

20 drops citronella essential oil

Spray around you & on yourself.

OPTION 2
GERANIUM LAVENDER

In a BPA-free spray bottle, mix:

4 oz distilled water

5 drops geranium essential oil

10 drops lavender essential oil

20 drops citronella essential oil

Spray around you & on yourself.

OPTION 3
BASIL LEMON

In a BPA-free spray bottle, mix:

4 oz distilled water

5 drops lemon essential oil

10 drops basil essential oil

20 drops citronella essential oil

Spray around you & on yourself.

FLY REPELLANT: Flies hate bay leaves, lavender, mint and rosemary
- Put bay leaves and rosemary in a bowl and place it on kitchen counters, around garbage, or whenever you have flies.
- Mix 25 drops mint essential oil in 4 oz of water and spray in the house.
- Plant fresh lavender around the foundation of the house.

BEST SPIDER REPELLANT: Spiders hate peppermint!
- Add 10-15 drops of peppermint essential oil into a spray bottle with 4 oz of distilled water.
- Spray around door frames, windows, small cracks, corners of the ceilings and bathrooms.
- Use peppermint essential oil without water for an even more potent version.

ANT REPELLANT: Ants hate cinnamon, garlic and mint!
- Ants have a strong sense of smell. Place cinnamon essential oil and peeled sliced garlic around window tracks or holes. Replace the garlic every 3 days until ants are gone.
- Plant fresh mint around the foundation of the house.
- Wash away ant paths & trails with equal parts water and white distilled vinegar to confuse them.

'POO-POURRI' FREEDOM
spritz sprays

Basic Ingredients:
- **2 oz distilled water**
- **1 tsp witch hazel**
- **one of these EO blends**

Pour the distilled water into a spray bottle.
Add the witch hazel, and then your essential oils.
Cap the bottle, shake very well, and allow it to sit for a few hours before using.

Deodorizing Room Spray
- **6 drops Bergamot EO**
- **2 drops Lemon EO**
- **1 drop Eucalyptus EO**

Apple Pie Spice Room Air Freshener
- **6 drops Cinnamon EO**
- **3 drops Cloves EO**

Orange Spice Room Air Freshener
- **5 drops Orange EO**
- **2 drops Cinnamon EO**

Stress Reliever Air Freshener Spray
- **4 drops Lavender EO**
- **3 drops Rose EO**
- **2 drops Clary Sage EO** (optional)

Mood Lifter Air Freshener Spray
- **4 drops Chamomille EO**
- **3 drops Orange EO**
- **2 drops Ylang Ylang EO**

Sleepy-Hour Relaxation Air Freshener Spray
- **4 drops Lavender EO**
- **3 drops Chamomille EO**

Pet Deodorizing Room Spray
- **6 drops Cedarwood EO**
- **3 drops Tea Tree EO**

Tip for the bathroom: *Add 6 drops of eucalyptus, purification, or peppermint EO into a spray bottle. Add the witch hazel and distilled water. A light mist before doing your business works FAR better than air fresheners... and it's chemical-free!*

FRANKINCENSE & MYRRH
Body Butter

INGREDIENTS

1 cup Organic shea butter
1/4 cup Organic aloe butter
1/4 cup Organic palm oil
1/2 cup Organic coconut oil
2 teaspoon jojoba oil

20 drops Myrrh EO
20 drops Frankincense EO
15 drops Orange EO
20 drops Elemi EO
25 drops Ylang Ylang EO

INSTRUCTIONS

In double boiler or crock pot, combine all ingredients <u>except essential oils</u>.

Stir till all ingredients are melted (do not overheat).

Remove from heat & let cool slightly.

Add essential oils of choice.

Move to fridge & let stand approximately 1 hour until it starts to somewhat harder.

Use a hand mixer to whip for no less than 10 minutes and can take up to 30 minutes of beating. It will begin to get fluffy (change to a white colour and solidify.

Scoop into dark glass containers.

Keep in a cool place & use within 6 months or less.

Properties of Frankincense
Anti-catarrhal, anti-cancer, antiseptic, anti-tumorous, expectorant, anti-depressant, immune stimulant, sedative, helps slow the aging process, keeps skin youthful, helps diminish scarring, apply on wounds, scrapes & warts.

Properties of Myrrh
Anti-infectious, anti-inflammatory,antiseptic,anti-tumorous, astringent, tonic, helps with inflammation, skin allergies, cracked skin, impetigo, stretch marks, vaginal thrush, eczema, fungal infection, ringworm, wrinkles, helps promote spiritual awareness & is uplifting. MYRRH is a TRUE GIFT - when we open our hearts & minds to receive gifts, they will be given.

Properties of Orange
Anti-depressant, anti-cancer, antiseptic, anti-spasmodic, digestive, sedative & tonic, can be used for anxiety, calming, constipation, indigestion, oily skin, insomnia. ORANGE brings peace & happiness to mind, body & joy to the heart.

Properties of Elemi (poor mans Frankincense)
Anti-depressant, anti-infectious, antiseptic, expectorant, sedative, can help with chapped skin, rashes, allergies, tissue repair, emotional & spiritual support.

Properties of Ylang Ylang
Anti-depressant, antiseptic,anti-spasmodic, sedative & tonic, can help with hair loss & split ends, mental fatigue, stress, tension, have calming effect, soothe insect bites, can lower blood pressure, calm rapid breathing, anxiety, can help balance heart function, intestinal problems, libido issues, skin problems.

How to make...
THIEVES DIY
Foaming hand soap

1/3 cup Castile Soap
10-15 drops of Thieves essential oil
5 drops Lemon essential oil
1 clear plastic bottle with White Foamer Pump

Add Castile Soap to bottle and then add EOs.
Fill slowly with water and you're done!

You can also choose to add 1-2 drops of Vitamin E to the mix.

HEALTHY HAIR
Spritzer

In a 2 oz spray bottle, add:

10 drops Lavender essential oil
10 drops Cedarwood essential oil
10 drops Rosemary essential oil
10 drops Frankincense essential oil
1 oz witch hazel
a pinch of Himalayan salt

Top with distilled water. Shake to mix well.

Simply spray on root area twice daily to promote healthy hair and support regrowth.

DIY Medium-Hold Hair Spritz

Start with:
1/2 cup bottled water
5 tbsp organic Cane Sugar

Boil water and sugar, then allow to cool before adding:
1/2 cup Vodka

Note: essential oils used in this recipe support hair growth and healthier hair.

Next, add Young Living EO:
30 drops Frankincense
30 drops Cedarwood
30 drops Lavender
30 drops Rosemary

Stir and pour into a spritzer bottle. Be sure to Spritz lightly and wait a couple minutes until hair is dry and style is set.

Bath Bomb Recipe

Dry Mix

1 Cup of Baking Soda
1/2 Cup of Epsom Salt
1/2 Cup of Arrow Root
1/2 Cup of Citric Acid

In a separate bowl, mix the following ingredients:

30 drops of your favourite essential oils (any combination that add to 30 drops in total)
3 Tbsp of olive oil

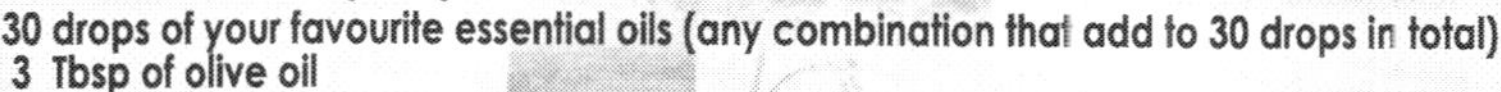

VERY SLOWLY in small droplets, drop by drop, add the above oil mixture to the dry mix. Not too much at a time as not to activate the mix too much. Use a whisk to mix in the wet mix. You can also use a handheld blender.

NEXT: Fill a spray bottle full of water. Set it to light mist. Spray the dry mix 2-3 times then whisk or blend.

Keep repeating this process till the mixture feels like damp wet sand. Be careful not to add too much water as not to activate the bath bomb mixture allowing it to fizz. Spray just enough water to make it stick together when compressing.

Put in molds to compress. Compressing the mix is key so it sticks together. You have the option to leave it in the mold to hold it together or take it out. Leave it overnight to thoroughly dry to ensure the bath bombs get hard before use.

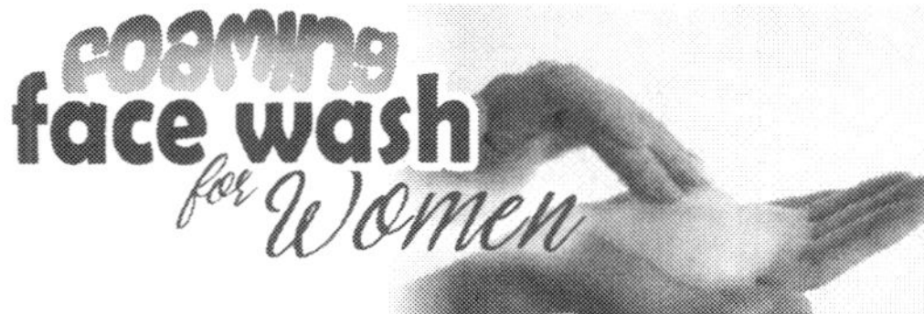

foaming face wash for Women

3/4 cup distilled water
2½ Tbsp unscented Castile soap
1 tsp vitamin E oil
1/2 tsp sweet almond oil
5 drops Frankincense essential oil
5 drops Geranium essential oil
Foaming soap dispenser

This Foaming Face Wash recipe leaves your skin soft and smooth, and clean without over drying. The recipe 'for Women' is perfect for beautifying skin of all ages and leaves a healthy glow. The vitamin E and almond oil work together to protect and nourish dry or mature skin that needs extra moisturizing.

Add all the ingredients into your foaming soap dispenser, stirring to combine well. To use, dispense one pump into your hand or use a facial scrubber. Rub over your face and rinse with water.

Note: other essential oils like Rose, Lavender, Myrrh, Rosemary and Elemi can be substituted to this recipe.

Lip Balm **recipe**

Ingredients:

3 heaping Tbsp beeswax chips
1/2 cup Shea butter
1/4 cup coconut oil
1/4 cup your choice of organic carrier oil
(jojoba, apricot, sunflower, grapeseed, or olive oil)
1/8 tsp vitamin E
1/8 tsp of castor oil (adds shine to the lip balm)
40 drops of your favourite YL oils

Examples of Essential Oils to use:
Lavender & Orange
Citrus Fresh & Lemon
Orange & Cinnamon Bark
Peppermint & Orange
Grapefruit
Lime

DILUTION is important for Essential Oils. 1-5% is recommended for daily skin care and daily use. 5-6 drops of oils per ounce of carrier oil. (this recipe is approximately 1% dilution)

In a small slow cooker or small pot on low heat, melt the beeswax. Add the butters until completely melted - do not overheat. Next add the carrier oil, vitamin E & castor oil. Allow the mixture to cool slightly before adding your essential oils. Pour into tins or tubes and let harden.

3 Ingredient FACE & LIP *scrub*

1 tbsp Brown Sugar
1 tbsp Coconut Oil
1 tbsp Organic Honey

Mix the ingredients together in a bowl. Apply to your face with clean fingers. Rub gently in a circular motion for about 2 minutes. If a little falls in your mouth from your lips,.. enjoy the taste!

Cracked Heel Salve

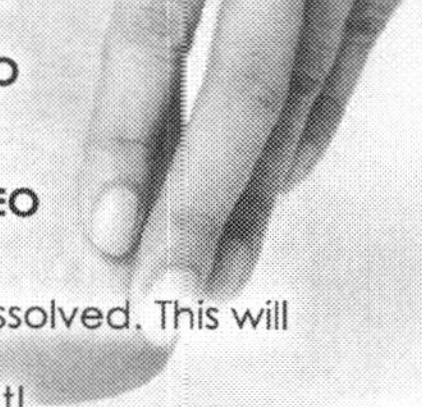

3 Tbsp beeswax
1/4 cup shea butter
1/4 cup coconut oil
1/4 cup magnesium flakes dissolved in
2 Tbsp boiling water
(or 1/4 cup pre-made magnesium oil)

10 drops each of:
- Oregano EO
- Peppermint EO
- Lavendar EO
- Myrrh EO
- Sandalwood EO
- Geranium EO

Pour 2 Tbsp boiling water into magnesium flakes and stir until dissolved. This will create a thick liquid. Set aside to cool.
Put beeswax in a pot and melt over stove. Do not use high heat!
Add coconut oil and shea butter. Stir just until all is melted.
Add dissolved magnesium mixture to the oil mixture, slowly mixing until well blended.
Add the essential oils.

Put in fridge 20-25 minutes until cold but not thickening.
Beat 20-30 minutes with beater until it reaches a body butter consistency.
Apply to cracked heels every night. I love to apply this to my feet every night for good feet maintenance - some TLC for your tootsies!

[note: will keep in fridge up to 6 months]

Hydrating Hand & Foot Cream

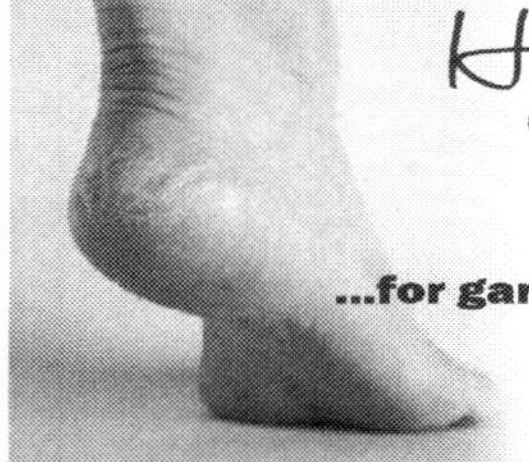

...for garden hands and flip-flop feet

1/4 cup shea buter
1/8 cup sweet almond oil
1 Tbsp beeswax
10 drops Frankincense EO
10 drops Lavender EO
10 drops Myrrh EO

Melt the shea butter, beeswax and sweet almond oil together in a double boiler (or you can just use a Pyrex measuring cup and place it in a pot of simmering water). Stir the mixture as it melts. Once everything is melted, remove it from the heat and allow it to cool for 5-10 minutes.

Stir in the essential oils and pour the liquid hand cream into a small glass container, and allow it to set overnight to infuse all the oils.

Apply this homemade moisturizing cream to your dry hands and feet as often as needed - especially after a long day working outside or playing in the dirt.

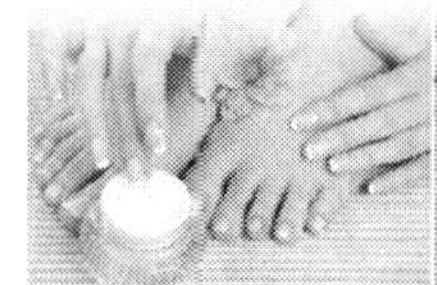
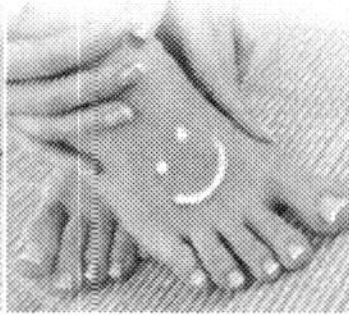

anti-aging *serum*

8 drops Neroli oil
8 drops Frankincense oil
6 drops Myrrh oil
4 drops Geranium oil
4 drops Helichrysum oil
4 drops Ylang Ylang oil
3 drops Lavender oil
3 drops Rose oil
2 drops Blue Tansy oil

Add your favourite carrier oil to fill a 10ml roller bottle.
Apply to face morning and night after cleansing.

Rejuvinating EYE *serum*

In a 10ml roller ball, add:
3 drops Frankincense EO
3 drops Lavender EO
2 drops Helichrysum EO
2 drops Carrot Seed EO
2 drops Lemon EO
2 drops Copaiba EO
Fill with Jojoba oil

Apply around your eyes every night before bed.

Essential Oils
in the **Shower**

For relief from asthma, cold, flu, or sinus congestion!

RC
Thieves
Peppermint
Eucalyptus
Raven
Mellisa
Tea Tree
Northern Lights Black Spruce

Lemongrass
Oregano
Rosemary
Immupower
En-r-gee
Majestic Canada

Add a few drops of essential oils to a washcloth and place it on the floor of the shower. When hot water hits the washcloth, the steam will release the essential oil vapors in the shower.

Use any of these essential oils separately or in combination.
Just 4-6 drops in total makes your shower smell like a spa!

FOR BATHING: Put 8 drops essential oils total combination into 1/2 cup Epsom Salts, run warm water and enjoy the spa treatment!

Mouthwash DIY recipe

1 cup of purified or distilled water
1/4 tsp salt
5-10 drops of Thieves EO (depends on how strong you want it)
4 drops of Peppermint EO
2 drops of Frankincense EO
1 tsp baking soda (optional)

Put the salt in a glass* bottle. Add the EOs to the salt. Add the water, and shake.

** essential oils can degrade plastic so glass is highly recommended*

Starter Kit
ROLL-ON BLENDS

Use a 10 ml roller ball. Top with your favourite carrier oil.

Sweet Dreams

10 drops Stress Away EO
15 drops Lavender EO

Happy Tummy

10 drops Peppermint EO
20 drops Digize EO

Just Chill

10 drops Frankincense EO
10 drops Copaiba EO
10 drops Stress Away EO

Deep Breath

10 drops Lemon EO
15 drops Raven EO
5 drops Peppermint EO

Ready To Work Out

20 drops Raven EO
10 drops Peppermint EO
10 drops Lemon EO

Happy Skin

10 drops Frankincense EO
10 drops Copaiba EO
10 drops Lavender EO

Be Well

15 drops Thieves EO
10 drops Frankincense EO
5 drops Lemon EO

Changing Seasons

8 drops Lavender EO
8 drops Lemon EO
8 drops Peppermint EO
8 drops Copaiba EO

Wake Up

15 drops Peppermint EO
15 drops Citrus Fresh EO

Infused Strawberry Lime Recipe

Perfect for a hot summer day!

In a 2 quart pitcher, combine:
1 cup strawberries, sliced
2 limes, sliced
6-8 drops YL Lime Plus/Vitality EO
**2-4 drops YL Spearmint Plus/Vitality
or Peppermint Plus/Vitality EO**
Sparkling water

Add ice, stir and enjoy!

Infused Organic Green Tea Recipe

Steep 2 quarts Organic Green Tea.

Cool the tea and pour it into a large
pitcher. Then add:
1 lemon, sliced
1 lime, sliced
5 drops YL Lemon Plus/Vitality EO
3 drops YL Lime Plus/Vitality EO
2 drops YL Peppermint Plus/Vitality EO

Add ice, stir and enjoy!

Herb Cheese Ball Spread

2 ½ cups sharp white cheddar
2 – 8oz pkgs cream cheese softened
2 Tbsp fresh chives chopped

Mix together cheeses and chives. Add:
1 drop Marjoram+ EO
1 drop Sage+ EO
1 drop Black Pepper+ EO

Add extra oil if more flavour is desired.
Chill for one hour.

Form into a big ball and roll onto
crushed nuts to coat.
Chill overnight and serve with
crackers and fruit.

Organic Dill Veggie Spread

8 oz organic sour cream
3 Tbsp chives chopped
2 Tbsp dill finely chopped
Pinch of sea salt
5 drop Dill+ EO
1 drop Black Pepper+ EO

Mix well, serve in one hour with
organic veggies.

Store in refrigerator.

Lemon Basil Salad Dressing

½ cup organic cold press olive oil
1-2 cloves garlic crushed
¼ tsp sea salt
2 tsp basil chopped
2 drops Lemon+ EO
1 drop Basil+ EO

Mix all ingredients in a glass jar and shake well.
Let it sit for 4 hours for flavours to meld.

Note: the zest or juice of one lemon, lime or orange can be replaced with approximately 1-2 drops of the same flavour EO

French Bread Dipping Oil

½ cup organic cold press olive oil
¼ tsp balsamic vinegar
1 drop Oregano+ EO
1 drop Thyme+ EO
1 drop Basil+ EO
1 drop Rosemary+ EO

Mix well and serve with baguettes or French bread.

Note: recipes that call for 1 Tbsp of Oregano, Thyme, fennel, coriander, etc can be replaced with ½ - 1 drop of the essential oil pending personal taste

Best Ever Guacamole

2 avocados mashed
1-2 clove garlic crushed
2 Tbsp chopped red onion
2 Roma tomatoes seeded & diced
1 Tbsp fresh cilantro chopped
2-3 drops Lime+ EO
Pinch of sea salt

Mix all ingredients together & enjoy!

Note: 1 tsp = approx 80 drops of an essential oil

Grilling Marinade

Excellent on chicken or fish!

2 lbs meat of choice
¾ cup organic cold press olive oil
½ cup soy sauce
2 Tbsp crushed onion
2 drops Orange+ EO
3 drops Lemon+ EO
1 drop Ginger EO

Mix well and let stand 1 hour.

Pour over meat and let stand overnight. BBQ or bake in over. So good!

Chapter 12

Healing with Crystals

Albert Einstein said it best, " Everything is energy." We literally live in a sea of vibration. Therefore, if you think crystals have healing potential, the positive vibes of the stone will amplify those thoughts. Four out of our five senses – sight, sound, touch, and taste – receive sensory input from the environment which is transferred through our nervous system to the brain. Everything has a frequency. To put frequency in perspective, dead foods such as hamburger and chicken have a frequency of 3 to 5 MHz; raw almonds vibrate at 50 MHz. Living greens such as broccoli, spinach, and wheatgrass have a frequency of 70 MHz.

Technology shows us that a healthy human body has a frequency of 62 to 70 MHz. When you have a cold or flu it drops down to 58 MHz. The frequency of a body with cancer, is at 42 MHz and when the death process begins, the frequency is measured at 20 MHz.

Like essential oils, crystals also have healing energies. According to researchers in Washington using Taino technology, the vibrational frequencies are the highest of any natural substance known to man. Higher frequencies in essential oils or crystals can ultimately raise the human vibrational frequency.

Crystals vibrate at different frequencies, depending on their matter, size, thickness and energy. Because there are so many variables in the crystal stones no two are alike, so a certain frequency cannot be assigned to a particular amethyst or rose quartz or any other crystal. Many years have been spent researching healing crystals and how they are used for different issues; many are powerful and can create a kundalini syndrome and detox reactions like headaches, emotional duress, and lethargy. They all have beautiful energies – a gift from planet Earth.

Crystals come in every size, shape and color; some are multicoloured. All crystals and gemstones are living organisms, have a life energy of their own, and are alive and usually grow in clusters. Many are as old as our planet; clear quartz has been on earth since the beginning of time and ancient civilizations have used crystals as protection, peace offerings, and jewelry. Today quartz makes up 12% of the earth's crust and is used in almost every kind of technology, including time keeping, electronics, and information storage. If it's possible for crystals to communicate through computer chips, how amazing that their connection to earth and its life-giving elements, actually have vibrational energy. That energy helps universal healing which can clear CHAKRA blockages and ward off negative energy.

Harnessing the energy of the sun, the moon and the oceans, semi-precious stones connect us to earth as soon as we come into contact with them. It takes a conscious effort to open your heart and mind to the power of crystal healing. Our first experiences with crystals left us both in awe of their powers. Both Marty and I had crystals laid beside the different chakras on our bodies and after half hour or so, the stones were very, very warm. They were not touching our bodies directly, so it was amazing that they drew so much energy. Being it was our first experience with them, it not only fascinated us, but we continued to work with their energy, clearing blockages and leaving a peaceful grounded feeling of wellness. Chronically ill patients can have anxiety and fear of end times. Crystal healing can bridge the gap between earth and the spiritual world, help connecting them to God, the universe and peace.

Selecting personal crystals will seem as though they call you; the crystal will catch your eye and when you hold it, you will feel a connection of frequency in this magical world of vibrations. Crystal energy helps you on your spiritual journey because it works to hold your intention and reminds you of your connection to earth. A well thought out intention is the starting point for healing crystals because specific intentions instilled into your daily thought patterns also become part of the energy.

One of the first pieces of scientific evidence relating to the power of crystals was work done by a brilliant scientist, Marcel Vogel, who worked at IBM Research Centre for twenty-seven years. He noticed their shape took the form of what he was thinking while he was watching them grow. He hypothesized that these vibrations are the result of constant assembling and disassembling of bonds between molecules. He also tested metaphysical power of quartz crystal and proved that rocks can store thoughts similar to how tapes use magnetic energy to record sound. He had over 100 patents, but the most famous is now known as the Vogel-cut crystal instrument used to store, amplify, convert, and cohere subtle energies. To research more on Vogel's world changing work, Google "vogelcrystals.net".

Healing crystals remind us to quiet the mind's chatter and connect to the universally healing vibrations of the earth. The technique of using gemstones and crystals on the receiver's body for healing is called laying of the stones. It is a powerful method of cleansing negative energy, clearing and balancing the chakras, releasing emotions, and bringing light and healing into all the body meridians. The dedicated stones move the receiver's vibration into alignment with the universe, transforming wellness, and grounding into the earth.

Finding the right stones is like any practice of wellness. It requires patience while you quiet the mind and realign the mind and body balance. If you notice hot or cold sensations, pulsations, or calmness and tranquility, these are all signs that particular crystal is perfect for your healing needs. Whether you are seeking a crystal for its physical beauty, or bringing peace, happiness, or tranquility into your life, crystals all work to increase your vibrational frequency.

Thoughts create vibrations throughout the universe, so having a clear insight into your aspirations, dreams, and purpose is crucial that you do not get caught up in negative thought patterns. Intentions are like magnets, they attract what will make them come true, so set your intentions by setting goals that align with your end goal result. Crystals want to work for you, but you have to tell them what job and purpose you need them to do. The most important thing to remember when working with your crystals, is to give yourself time to sync with the energy of your crystals, put in a positive mindset and be sure of the intentions you want your crystals to do. You can get crystals for meditation, prosperity, wellness, abundance, and new opportunities.

Finding the right crystal therapist is as important as finding the right crystal. I would look for someone who resonates with your soul, exceptionally beautiful in every way, caring, spiritual, intuitive, kind-hearted, helpful, gentle, and spiritually connected. Be sure to ask for credible references, and research your options. Being comfortable with your therapist is a huge part of the healing process.

Cleansing and recharging your crystals are as important as learning to use them. My good friend Tula Manning, a Certified International Master Crystal Therapist, has given me information to share with you because what books teach may not be true. You can find more valuable information at www.crystalempowerments.com.

Once you have chosen your precious crystals, you have to remove all programs, intentions, and stale energies that the crystal may have picked up possibly right from the mine itself or from being where people touched the crystal and would have interfered with its energies. Usually you can tell a crystal needs cleaning just by looking at it. It should sparkle and not be sticky. If you run your finger over it and find it is sticky or feels heavy to wear, it needs a vacation in a salt spa. When your crystal jewellery - rings, pendants, bracelets - are out with you all day long, exposed and working in a hostile environment, they need some TLC. The Sioux Indians teach that jewelry should be cleansed before bedtime in a bowl of salt water, then they are up and ready to go when you are.

Start with the removal of all programs as soon as you bring the crystal home. Sit in a quiet place, clear your to-do list and centre yourself; take a few deep breaths and relax. Start your sage burner and run the crystal back and forth through the smoke saying, "I CLEANSE THIS CRYSTAL OF ALL-NEGATIVE LOW VIBRATIONS. I REMOVE ALL PREVIOUS PROGRAMS AND INTENTIONS, RE-INSTATING THIS CRYSTAL TO ITS NATURAL GLORY SO IT MAY RELEASE ITS SUBTLE ENERGIES FOR THE GREATEST GOOD OF ALL."

If you want to keep the program that is already in the crystal, you would still run it through the smoke saying, "I CLEANSE THIS CRYSTAL OF ALL NEGATIVE, LOW VIBRATIONS, KEEPING THE INTEGRITY AND THE INTENT OF THE PREVIOUS PROGRAM INTACT."

The next step is to prepare one tablespoon of Himalayan salt per litre of warm water in a glass dish. Like the essential oils, crystals do not like plastic. Place some sage and the crystal in the water for twenty minutes. You can bathe more than one crystal at a time. You could place the crystals in an Amethyst Geode or on a cluster just to make sure that there is nothing left on the crystal that might have been missed. Generally if you used the sage and salt bath, your crystal is now ready for charging, infusing them with energy. Do not soak Selenite, Kyanite, Dessert rose, Pearls, Celestite, or Angelita as they will dissolve when extremely wet.

PLEASE DO NOT PLACE YOUR CRYSTALS IN THE SUNLIGHT. Most crystals were not formed in the sunlight itself except for Amber, therefore prefer the dark. Sunlight will burn them or fade them, and the reflection can cause a fire. Treat crystals as you would your skin. To charge crystals, ideally a full moon is recommended, but placing them in the night is acceptable. Placing them on your windowsill will work but putting them outside is the preferred method. Positioning them three days before the full or new moon will have a greater impact, as these energies are far greater than after the moon cycle. All moon beams will energize your crystals; some crystals that work harder may need a full moon vacation.

Crystals love to work, so now give them a job to do. Once you figured out what you want to program into the crystal, sit in a quiet place and hold the crystal in your hand. Either hand works. The sensations you feel may be different, but programming is key to having your crystal work for you.

Close your eyes and feel the energy of your crystal. It may be a cold or hot feeling, a tingling feeling like a little electric shock, or just knowing you have a bond. With that you then say, "I DEDICATE THIS CRYSTAL TO THE HIGHEST GOOD OF ALL; MAY IT BE USED IN LIGHT AND LOVE. I ASK THAT THIS CRYTAL BE PROGRAMMED AS A SACRED HEALING TOOL TO CARRY THE PROGRAM [fill in your requests]. I RESPECT AND THANK THE CRYSTAL DEVA FOR GRANTING THIS REQUEST."

Your crystal is now ready to go. Carry it with you, place it under your pillow, meditate with it, keep it in different corners of your house, your car, and at your work place. Crystals do not need to sit close to work effectively. Your energy field extends about three feet around you, so do not hesitate to work on your entire aura when using crystals. Whatever you program into your crystal, as long as you are from light, love, and respect, it will work for you. Enjoy every moment you spend with your crystal and appreciate that it is helping you. The more you work and keep the same program in the crystal, the stronger it becomes.

Crystals can be powerful in achieving your goals. Whether you carry them in a bag, put them in your handbag or purse, place them on your night stand or behind your computer at work, keep small crystals in your bra or wear them as a piece of jewellery, do not worry if you lose them. Pink crystals have their own spirit, so if you lose one, it means you no longer need it. Crystals can have a strong impact and can do many things quickly, especially if you are very open to them. Trust the crystal's energy and pay attention to sensations, feelings, images, memories, or thoughts. Many people are rediscovering the immense power of stones for improving health and well-being on many different levels: mind, body, spirit, and beyond.

Believe it and you will see it.

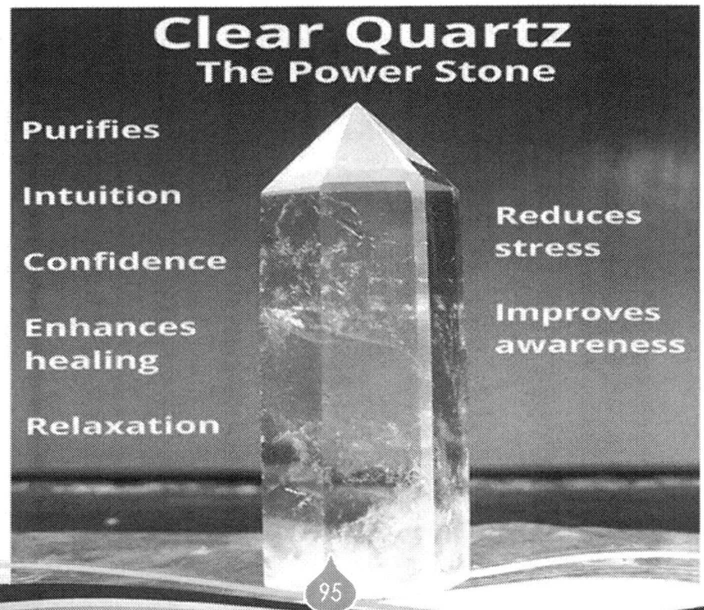

Healing Crystals for 10 Different Cancers

1. **Rose Quartz** - for breast cancer: pink and heart are synonymous with breast cancer crystals. It can lower stress, clear out anger, jealousy and resentment of others, allowing the healing of disease associated emotions.

2. **Hematite** - has powerful energy to displace or dissolve malignant brain tumours. It can work effectively in diminishing the physical pain. When it's programmed by keeping on the Third Eye or Chakra, hematite detoxifies the brain cells with anti-inflammatory powers.

3. **Amethyst** - is a general healer of cancer, immune booster, and a stone of balance. It inhibits the growth of cancer cells faster than most healing crystals. Amethyst is a blood cleaner and dissipates pain.

4. **Carnelian (and Bloodstone)** - are an effective combination of healing the liver and kidneys. Together Carnelian and Bloodstone are workhorses that can assist in healing blood cancers such as leukemia, skin cancers and blood rich organs. Carnelian transmutes and cleanses negative energy, making it an effective cancer stone.

5. **Red Aventurine** - colon cancer requires a heavy detox and fortification of the immune system. If your colon cancer is in the first stage, red aventurine can help you fight it from spreading. It is an anti-inflammatory and can also be used to treat cancers of the abdomen.

6. **Amber** - to heal the elimination organs of your body, omnipotent crystal vibrations are necessary to penetrate the liver tissues and heal from within. It can stop the pain and help regenerate the cells to form a healthier liver by rejuvenation of the cells and tissues, helping the body heal itself.

7. **Smoky Quartz** - healing almost all lower chakra disorders, smoky quartz reduces physical and mental damage due to cancerous growth in your ovaries. It has additional properties of assisting in the treatment of radiation sickness and after effects of chemotherapy. The darker the crystal, the more effective it is known to be. It absorbs negative energy, radiation and anything that is a toxin to the body.

8. **Malachite** - is the most underused healing stone. It pinpoints tumours and growths, correcting the DNA and cellular structures that cause cancer. It can be used on all forms of cancer and stimulates the immune system.

9. **Larimar** - is a stone for those who are pro-active in healing. Larimar is exceptional for cancer that has invaded the lymph nodes and lymph system. It is particularly healing for mouth, throat, head, neck and chest. Placed over the point of pain it will draw it out and placed over the site of the disease Larimar will pinpoint the illness to direct healing.

10. **Emerald** - is important in detoxifying, repairing and boosting the immune system, and a healer of the chest cavity and spine. It is said it can heal any malignant condition. It is very effective in eye disorders and cancer of the eyes. It is a stone you can depend on to seek and destroy any infectious conditions.

There are many other crystals that can be helpful in your cancer battle such as JADE for kidney, liver and prostrate, and CITRINE best for chemotherapy side effects. It can activate your aura energies to communicate with the higher selves for healing. GREEN AVENTURINE can help by engulfing the pain of the cancerous life. It's anti-inflammatory properties benefit the thymus gland and the nervous system. This stone is powerful enough to erase the sadness from the cancer patient and fill it with a sea of happiness. It works by clearing out the blocked energy which is growing as a tumour within your body. SELENITE, renowned as the light crystal, brings home the healing powers of divination. You can program Selenite to heal all kinds of cancer. Prominently used on the crown chakra, it can keep tumours and symptoms of cancer away from you.

Crystals, like essential oils, are there for extra support and never meant to avoid your doctor's advice or treatments. When you combine holistic methods, it can only make your fight more powerful, and empowerment is healing.

ONYX
* Cleanses the air
* Rids your home of negative energy

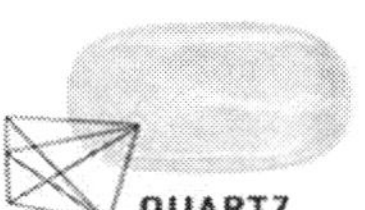

QUARTZ
* Helps relieve stress and frustration
* Eases anxiety

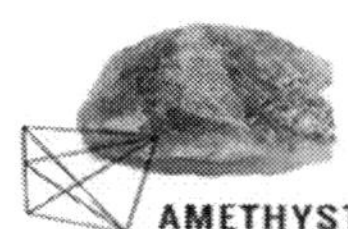

AMETHYST
* Helps relieve headaches and fatigue
* Promotes good dreams and good skin Supports bones, joints

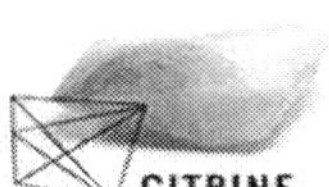

CITRINE
* Use to boost concentration
* Boost memory
* Spark creativity

LAPIS LAZULI
* A touted ancient migraine remedy
* Supports the immune system

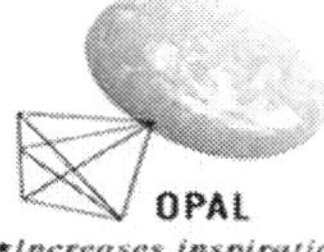

OPAL
* Increases inspiration and creativity
* Helps with PMS and headaches

TOPAZ
* Works to balance hormones & combat aging

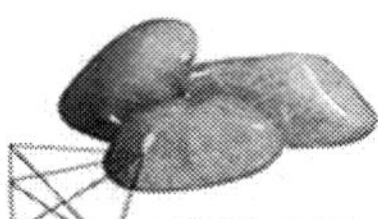

AQUAMARINE
* Aids with acid reflux and gastrointestinal disorders

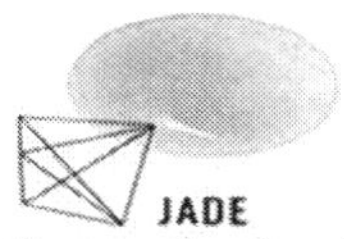

JADE
* Supports the adrenal glands and relieves headaches

GARNET
* Good for back pain, calcium deficiencies and tissue regeneration

BLOODSTONE
* Helps regulate blood pressure & supports the circulatory system
* Good for colds

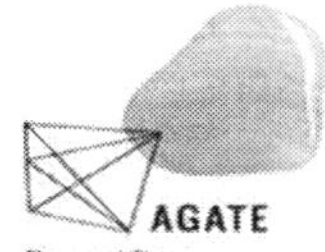

AGATE
* Detoxifies
* Eases anxiety

Meditation Prayer

Lord, make me an instrument of Thy peace;
Where there is hatred, let me sow Love; Where there is injury, Pardon;
Where there is doubt, Faith; Where there is despair, Hope;
Where there is darkness, Light; Where there is sadness, Joy.

Lord, grant that I may not seek to be consoled as to console;
To be understood as to understand; To be loved as to love.
For it is in the giving that we receive; It is in the pardoning that we are pardoned;
And it is in dying that we are born to eternal life.

Chapter 13

Body, Mind and Soul - Feeding the Soul

Cancer should always be treated by first discovering the underlying emotions that may have contributed to the onset of the disease. Raw, negative emotions over time, can not only trigger cancer but can further its metastasis.

Negative emotions like anger, fear, helplessness, thoughts of abandonment, insecurity, losses and deep-rooted grief can keep you in a suffering state. Emotional and spiritual feelings and attitudes that negatively impact one's life are perhaps the most difficult to recognize. Negative emotions can be a precursor to both mental and the physical dysfunction of the body, leading to chronic disease including cancer.

Depression, low energy, being judgmental, low self-esteem, having few or no goals and little to no motivation can cause a negative attitude. According to National Health Science Foundation, an average person has about 12,000 to 60,000 thoughts per day. To that, 80% are negative, and 95% are repetitive. If we continue to repeat those negative thoughts, then we think negative more often than positive, and that can lead to health issues.

Your thoughts are the root of your destiny. Lao Tzu wrote, "Watch your thoughts; they become words. Watch your words; they become actions. Watch your actions; they become habit. Watch your habits; they become character. Watch your character; it becomes your destiny." Our positive and negative thoughts influence every single thing in our lives.

We learn so much about feeding our body proper nutrition, supplements, exercise and clean living; we feed our brains new challenges, brain mapping therapies, access bars and many other activities like puzzles, crossword games; but what about the soul? How do we feed the soul? How do we energize and tune into that great universal power to connect spiritually?

Our soul is what gives us our personality, and it's through our soul that we live our relationship with God or our higher power. It's in our spirit that we have meaning and purpose in life. It's our spirit that enables us to love one another, ourselves and God. It's through our spirit that we have communion and fellowship with God. Our spirit gives us intuition between right and wrong. Our spiritual pathways feed our soul. The interconnection between the spirit, the body and the soul are complex, but our spiritual health will have a great impact on our emotional health which will significantly impact our physical health. In 3 John 1:2, "Beloved, I pray that you prosper in all things and be in health, just as your soul prospers." This is an indication of the importance of attending to matters of the soul as it relates to being healthy.

If chronic stress is left unchecked, over some time our bodies will take a toll. A strong faith can help us cope with stress and enable that impact to be less significant. Without a strong personal faith, we must resort to our resources and often that leads to addiction and other methods of escape. That behaviour can further the effects of stress on our physical health. Our beliefs and attitudes, determined by our faith, will play a significant role in our thinking patterns, which in turn play a significant role in our emotional and physical health.

Dr. Christina Puchalski, from the George Washington Institute for Spirituality and Health, states that physicians must understand patients' history in the context of their spiritual beliefs and practices. Researchers found that provision of support for spiritual needs are viewed as extending beyond both essential health care needs and priorities. Illness, injury, trauma, death, grief, loss, pain, and suffering in any form can be overwhelming and soul-wrenching. Spiritual care is less about words and more about compassion and openness to the divine presence, sometimes in silence, and sometimes by a gentle touch with reassurance that we are not alone.

In his journey with cancer, my son connected often with the spiritual realm by grounding with nature, meditation, prayer, a prayer circle, spiritual healing and crystal healing. Peace and calm would come over him, his anxiety would leave, and he felt embraced in the presence of a higher power. Marty lost his infant daughter in 2012, and the grief, the loss, the anger all played a part in his health issues. She was his angel, giving him comfort and divine love.

There are many stories and books written about Angels, about their spiritual love, and that each one of us has a Guardian Angel. They are real spiritual beings who are servants of God and help carry out His commands. Angels are mentioned 108 times in the Old Testament and 165 times in the New Testament. Angels are essentially ministering spirits, that live in the higher planes where they bask in the glow of God's love at all times and can carry that love back down to earth and into our hearts. Angels' purpose is to spread love, and they do this by healing, protecting, guiding, so you can experience deep in your soul, that unconditional love that explodes in your heart. Healing courses, Spiritual healers, workshops, past life regression therapy, and meditation can help you strengthen your ability to contact and interact with angels.

Dr. Brian Weiss has some influential books out on this subject. They include Messages from The Masters, Mirrors of Time, and Miracles Happen. They may be helpful in healing your soul and bringing your consciousness to a higher level and better perspective of inner peace.

Daily Guide to Help Feed Your Soul

1. **Connect with GOD or your higher power** - our soul has three significant components: our mind, will and emotions. Our mind is the conscious part where we do our thinking and resonating and subconscious is where we hold our deep beliefs and attitudes. It's also where we have our feelings, our emotions, and retain our memories. Our will is what gives us the ability to make choices. God wants us to enjoy our time on earth. He participates in our lives, eager to see us face each day with grace and confidence, holding us up when the hard places on our journey threaten our ability to stand up. God is in your life whether you acknowledge Him or not. Food for the soul are those experiences that help you understand and strengthen your connection with God. Watching a show like The World of Nature is like seeing the miracle of life in slow motion. Observing the web of life and our interconnectedness with the universe, fills our spirit to overflowing, and once again we are awestruck by our creator. Talk to Him, chat it up, pray, he wants to hear from you. The only thing that matters is that it comes from your heart.

2. **Regularly do good deeds and expect nothing in return** - Empathy can increase your well-being. Generosity and doing good can make a mark on a physical level beyond relaxation. Scientists have determined that acts of kindness (referred to as helpers high) are associated with the release of oxytocin; a hormone best known for creating emotional bonds and also linked to heart health. Scrooge had his spirit reborn after he discovered the joy of good deeds.

3 **Practice gratitude** - and use the guide provided in the chapter 'GRATITUDE – 365 Days of Gratefulness'. Create a life of happiness and well-being by giving thanks. As we create gratitude, we create a positive ripple effect, like a stone thrown into the water. It can potentially satisfy some of our greatest desires for happiness, inner peace, health, and contentment. Relishing in what you have, what you know, who is in your life, the experiences that you have is a beautiful way the acknowledge the symphony of your life.

4 **Meditate** - because if you stay connected to your soul and remain happy, you will find your heart filled with positive emotions. Connecting with your soul fifteen minutes to half hour a day can help you live a more conscious, mindful, and healthy life. Find a space that defines peace, sit in a comfortable position with your eyes closed and breathe deeply from the belly 3–4 times. Go deep into space, ask your soul for guidance, inhale and exhale as you allow your body to sense the space and stillness.

5 **Connect with the Universe** – there are more stars than grains of sand on the beach; not only are we living in this universe, but the universe is living in us. Fate, destiny, past, future, and present, our outer physical form and our inner metaphysical form are all connected. "For every action there is an equal reaction," says Newton. Through religion and science man has been on a quest to seek answers as to how we are all connected. Do we have a soul speaking to us from within and acting as a link to the outer world? To believe the Creator is not separate or distant, but rather within us, we need to acknowledge that there is a higher power – a power greater than we are, a power that created it all. This power has many names; some call Him GOD, others The Great one, The Creator, The Supreme Power, and the Universal Father in Heaven. Quantum Physics tells us that everything is energy, everything vibrates, and our thoughts are comic waves with potent energy – we are all a sea filled with energy. Our thoughts matter since we are part of universal energy. Through meditation, we can reach a higher power and be one with the universe. There is a powerful book on this subject called A Course in Miracles that I strongly recommend – a foundation for inner peace.

6 **Connect with Nature** – walk barefoot in the sand, on the grass, and walk the beach catching the ocean waves. Sit by a waterfall and feel the mist cover your face. Look up at the sky; really look at the night sky when the stars are out, and the moon is bright. Take a drive in the countryside, hear the birds and the crickets sing. Connecting with the natural world calms our nervous system and quiets us enough to listen to our soul speak out our inner voice of wisdom and intuition. Whether it's in the woods, a park, a valley, or paddling barefoot on the sea, being surrounded by nature really kicks in your reset button and recharges the soul.

7 **Dream bigger** - dreams provide nourishment for the soul. Fight the good fight. Shed your fears, be inspired to get out there and do positive things. Do what makes you happy. Do not get saddled into mediocre positions. Be passionate. Happy fulfilled souls revel in their joy and happiness.

8 **Engage in music** - music soothes the soul. Listening to meditative music, symphony, Beethoven's violin, or nature's sounds can nourish the soul and give great comfort and peace.

9 **Breathe** - breathe in the fresh air. Close your eyes, breathe in for 9 seconds, hold for 4, breathe out for 7 seconds. Really take in the elements cf nature. Be still and listen. Breathing can awaken your senses and connect your mind to your body in a fuller consciousness.

10 **Essential Oils bath** - from ancient times, essential oils have been used for their physical, mental and emotionally elevating properties. Bathing in half cup natural Epsom salts and 8-10 drops of your favourite essential oil can help you relax and put you in a meditative state.

> **ROSE** essential oil can stimulate the mind and create a sense of well-being. Its beautiful fragrance is almost intoxicating, calming and relaxing.

> **GERANIUM** essential oil can help release negative memories and take you back to peaceful, joyful and pleasing moments. It can also help ease nervous tension, balance emotions, lift the spirit, foster peace, well-being and hope.

> **ELEMI** essential oil may help nervous exhaustion, and stress. During meditation, it may help to calm and align the chakras. It may also bring the mind, body, and spirit into alignment with each other. It's also known for psychologically balancing and strengthening the spiritual planes.

> **ANGELICA** essential oil may help one release and let go of negative feelings by bringing one's memory back to the point of origin before trauma and anger was experienced. It can give emotional stability.

> **MELISSA** essential oil has a delicate, delightful, lemony scent that is unique among essential oils, providing excellent support to both body and mind. It has been known to be calming, uplifting, and may balance emotions. It may also remove emotional blocks and instill a positive outlook on life.

> There are many other essential oils that can help you on your wellness journey. Many essential oils are mentioned throughout my book and the many ways they can help you achieve a pro-active healthy lifestyle.

Chapter 14

Gratitude - 365 Days of Gratefulness

Gratitude allows us to celebrate the present, fill our hearts with love, hope, kindness and is just good medicine for the soul. The Webster Dictionary defines gratitude as having a sense of thankfulness and that warm feeling that is from within. Thankfulness is different, in that it expresses appreciation of benefits received. When you feel gratitude, you're pleased by the results of something someone did for you, without feeling anxious about paying it back.

Some studies show that gratitude can lower depression, has been associated with lowering blood pressure, lessen chronic pain and extend longevity. It is challenging to practice gratitude in the face of tragedy, especially when your world is crumbling around you.

It took me several weeks to find anything to be grateful for after my son's passing. As the days passed to weeks and I saw the incredible impact he made on so many people in his short life, I began to write down all those things I was grateful for. Grateful for his legacy, grateful for the hundreds of pictures I have of him, grateful for having worked alongside him, grateful for all the holidays and special events we shared, and grateful for the time in the hospital with him. I realize how blessed I was in so many ways, and then I started to see past Marty, to the younger son, Bryan who also battled cancer for three years. So much good came from our family, not because of who we were, but because of the suffering both boys endured during their battle with cancer.

Their suffering brought on compassion for others, a deeper level of awareness to the small things in life, a new meaning and purpose for life, and mostly, gratitude for being alive. Our adversity, our sorrows, our affliction and ultimately our heartbreak, opened doors to a better understanding that life is indeed a gift, one we must be grateful for 365 days a year. It's about understanding that life owes you nothing, and nothing can be taken for granted.

Living your life with gratitude means choosing to focus your time and attention on what you appreciate, connecting with the wonderfully ordinary things, great and small that can often be taken for granted. Finding these things in the midst of despair, loss of a loved one, loss of a job or a relationship, battling chronic illness, or whatever your stormy seas may bring, being grateful for just one small thing every day – 365 days a year, can start the healing process and repair emotional bonds. The healing power of gratitude brings greater happiness, more positive thoughts and emotions, fewer aches and pain, better sleep, improved self-esteem and improved overall health.

Sometimes our inner negative critic is our worse offender, interfering with our feelings of gratitude. This inner critic can take us out of our present most beautiful day and keep us entirely in our head, where these negative thoughts make us see through rose-coloured glasses instead of a more compassionate real lens. Being mindful and respectful of others allows us a deeper understanding of gratefulness, grateful for a dreary day because life can get in the way and take you places you would rather not be, or just when you think you have hardships, someone else is battling worse. Just be grateful for being exactly where the universe wants you to be, find your small gift in your present place, and awaken your senses to experience a higher level of appreciation.

Through both of my sons' journeys with cancer, although different paths, I never let either of them walk it alone; that journey made me aware that beneath its negative surface, there is an opportunity for spiritual and emotional growth and deepening of my purpose. You cannot help but find new values, be more appreciative of small things, declutter in life what is not essential, become more compassionate for others, gain a new inner strength that becomes a power surge for more intense personal growth and live every day being grateful.

I believe that gratitude goes hand in hand with forgiveness. Holding on to negative emotions, holding a grudge, being stuck in an angry state, dwelling on wrong-doings, and carrying on second and third generation feuds can be very detrimental to your health. Forgiveness is liberating. It frees us from that negative attachment; it liberates us from the cycle of negativity and anger, allowing us to open our hearts to gratitude, happiness and love. Focusing on forgiveness, accepting gratitude as our attitude, clears a path for embracing forgiveness, and promotes peace of mind.

Forgiveness like gratitude is a process that does not happen overnight. Forgiving ourselves every day 365 days a year is just as important as being grateful 365 days a year. You will see considerable improvements in your health when you walk this talk.

Every yesterday is the past; the past is done, those things which we might beat ourselves up for happened. We cannot undo what we did to others or ourselves. Forgiving ourselves can be the door of emotional healing we are all looking for. All of us respond to situations with the skills we have, and the mind frame we are in at the time. Sometimes we act out of survival mode, or our sense of pride or self-esteem was fragmented; let it go, move on, forgive those who trespass and truly forgive yourself. Move on to loving yourself, think kind thoughts towards yourself, be your own best friend, move on past your mistakes, forgive yourself because you are so worth it.

13 Positive Prompt Thoughts

1. What did God Bless me with today?
2. My Faith is more significant than my fears.
3. I will embrace joy.
4. Today I seek peace.
5. Where there is hope, there is light.
6. When there is love, forgiveness follows.
7. Be kind to yourself; be kind to others.
8. Today I will smell the roses.
9. Smiles are happy thoughts.
10. Realize the past is the past.
11. Celebrate victories, big or small.
12. Live in faith.
13. Travel on; trust in God – your higher power.

GratitudeNotes

TODAY I AM GRATEFUL FOR

Date:

1.
2.
3.
4.
5.
6.
7.
8.
9.
10.

CURRENT CHALLENGE

I am learning from this...

PEOPLE I AM GRATEFUL FOR

TODAY I CHOOSE TO LOVE MYSELF BECAUSE

1.
2.
3.

Notes

Chapter 15:

Grief - Facing the Unexpected

GRIEF was something I never prepared myself for, and not sure something one can prepare for. The toughest day, for me, was the day my son passed away, November 28, 2019. The moments that followed took my breath away, my heart stopped beating, and the chain of emotions swept over me relentlessly, leaving me physically and emotionally numb with exhaustion. Those emotions turned me into an apocalypse zombie, unable to think, unable to process, unable to function, grief overwhelmed me, and the day slipped into the night.

As the days went by, I knew this: I would live another day regardless of the desire or the process to which I would need to refine it. I soon realized that the blur of the days, weeks and months that came and went, I needed to try to move forward and get back to my life, my new life, my new normal. I think the saying, "Behind this smile is a mom missing her son,' totally expresses simply what every day brings. The brain fog became my new normal. Living in a cloud, I experienced dysfunctions in focus, learning, and with that frustration the simple tasks and work became difficult. I made mistakes that would never have happened in my pre-loss. I could not believe I sent out parcels for Christmas to my team members and realized a day later I had forgotten to sign their enclosed cards. I sent them, perfectly blank. I was not sure whether an apology was necessary, but I messaged them the greeting I had intended to convey. Grief can send you places you never thought possible.

I use the essential oil Brain Power and find it helpful in keeping me focused. As time passes, I find that fog is lifting, and some days I nearly see clearly.

Grief can come from many situations: the death of a child is the worst and death of a pet a close second (I remember Oprah grieving endlessly for her two beloved dogs). She said those dogs were closer to her than any human as they went to work with her, slept with her, were with her 24/7.

Loss can be felt from an unexpected breakup in a relationship, and in chronic disease that wipes away the very being of yourself. Terminally ill patients can experience different stages of grief.

Many who have not experienced grief, tell you to do a change of scenery, find a new hobby, remind you that you are strong, and you will get over it. That my friends, I can tell you does not work. As I edit this book on the deck of my Mazatlán condo, I can say with absolute truth, the tears fell like rain, the memories continued to flood in, and the emotions continued to ride in, like the waves on the ocean, some surface waves, some wind-generated waves, and others become mountainous swells that eventually come to shore and disperse. So much energy needs to slowly be harnessed into good and positive.

I will share some things that are helping me get through the grieving process. I think for me, most importantly is embracing those who are near you, especially in the first two weeks of your loss. You truly know who your friends are and those who have your back at all times. Hold on dearly to the hugs, and words of encouragement from those who know what you are going through or those who have gone through their own grief journeys. It can be a lonely process, so keeping connected is essential to have a balance of peace and calm. Remember, no one will respond perfectly to your grief; even people you love can let you down.

Essential oils took the brunt of my emotional roller coaster and eased the edge of my anxiety. They work their magic for the turbulent emotions of sadness, despair, helplessness, rejection, anger, fear, insecurity, isolation, hopelessness, guilt, abandonment and loss. My favourite essential oil is Valor and I carry it everywhere with me, but spruce, sandalwood, cypress, rutavala, and the biblical essential oil combos like The Gift, Harmony, Release, OOLA Faith and Abundance all help care for ourselves mentally, emotionally, spiritually and physically. Essential oils are great to diffuse and wear topically.

Allow yourself to mourn, understand grief is normal, and know it's okay to be surprised by the intensity of your grief. Never make excuses if you have a meltdown in public, those who know you will understand, those that don't, do not matter. Grief does not move on a predictable path nor a fixed pace. It never goes out of your heart, but time does have a way of moving it to the background, kind of like the pictures you take on your iPhone. The pictures you took today of that beautiful sunset, suddenly are buried in hundreds more sunset pictures. As much as you try to bring those pictures back to the forefront, they soon get lost in the maze. The yearning for the person you lost never leaves you. It's okay to laugh, too, don't feel guilty for your positive emotions when dealing with loss.

You will ask the "WHY" more times than you thought possible, but that question rarely gets answered if at all. The "HOW" can help you live life more fully to honour your loved one. Moving on, honoring the memories you shared with those you lost, and more importantly, allow them to live in the legacy they left behind. A friend of mine set up a graduation scholarship award in her son's name, others hold a yearly fundraiser in memory of their son/brother, that gets donated to various local charities. Continuing your loved one's legacy is extremely healing.

My son Marty was a huge part of the Bryan Mudryk Golf Classic that raised $1.8 million for the Cross Cancer Institute. Together with my sons Marty and Bryan we were awarded a Philanthropy Award in 2013 and again in 2017. The money we raised was used to buy equipment at the Cross Cancer Hospital and some of that equipment was used for a few of Marty's tests.

Marty was president of Knight's Cabin, and together Marty and Rob Williams spearheaded the Williams & Mudryk 100 K Ride ... over $280,000 was raised for the Cross Cancer Institute and Knights Cabin, helping cancer patients directly with wellness care. I am very fortunate to be able to carry on Marty's legacy with my other son Bryan, our adopted- into-the family son Robby, the TSN and CTV families, all of our family and friends in a "Remembering Marty Wellness Night" and Williams & Mudryk 100 K Ride on JULY 12-13, 2019. Monies raised will be donated to Knight's Cabin and help facilitate wellness retreats for those in the cancer battle. I can focus on generating positive energy into helping others.

We had long chats several weeks before Marty passed away. He insisted that I continue my research, continue teaching, continue investing in myself, and do whatever it takes to get the wellness message out there. "People need to know," he said. "They need to be proactive. Illness is not an option." I am grateful for his encouragement because as I pen this, I pray that this message gets out there, and his legacy will live on in everyone who made some simple lifestyle changes towards better health.

Grief comes in waves. No matter how bad a day feels, it's only a day; you may go to sleep crying, but you wake up okay. One hour may be fine, the next may not; learn to go with the flow of your heart. Be kind to yourself. Eat healthily, work out, connect with nature, connect with your spiritual side. Your loved one is near. Balance busy because busy-busy will not make grief go away, nor will it let you think less about it. Take time to heal and process your journey. Walk alongside it and be amazed at what t can teach you. Try to embrace change and grow because of it.

Liquor, drugs, sex, work, etc. will not take the pain away. If you are using any of these to numb the pain, things will get worse. Never be afraid to seek help. Insomnia is a symptom of grief and can take weeks/months to get sleep patterns back to normal. My go-to are essential oils that I bathe and lather in — my tools that are slowly bringing back my ability to sleep through at least five hours straight. That has taken seven weeks to date, but some nights, like a day's grief comes in waves and not every night is restful. I see improvements.

Keep a journal, a blog, a memoir, write down your thoughts, things about your loved one you do not want to forget, some happy memories, your expression of their loss and how that has affected you. By keeping a journal, you maintain a bond with your loved one. I was fortunate to spend time with my son in the hospital and our last words to each other were, "I LOVE YOU."

If you never had an opportunity to say goodbye, write them a letter; it's your chance now, your way. I had a Christmas card to give Marty in the hospital, but he insisted he would be home for Christmas and would open it then. That never happened, so on Christmas Day, I opened it and read it to him. It was my way of saying I miss you, Merry Christmas. Sometimes the why never gets answered.

Rely on your faith, not necessarily a church or religion, but your own connection with a greater power, your GOD. Feeling grateful was the hardest thing I could do in the wake of losing my son. But slowly I saw so many things in my life that he changed for the better and I was grateful for that. I saw many things he changed in people's lives. They shared their stories of what Marty meant to them, and for that I was grateful. Each day, write down the things that bring you joy, even the small things you are thankful for. Gratitude heals at a very deep level.

Essential Oils for Grief

I am genuinely grateful for having essential oils in my home to diffuse and topically apply. They have been so helpful in getting me through the worse days and nights when grief overwhelms me. I have used these oils, depending on the emotion I was experiencing and which feeling with which I was struggling.

Oils resonate differently with everyone, and I strongly recommend you try the ones that the smell pleases you. Essential oils can help dissolve some of the roller coaster of sadness, helplessness, fear, isolation, guilt, plus much more. Oils work very quickly by stimulating the olfactory system, which is connected directly to the nose and the brain. Oils can calm, banish brain fog, recharge your feelings of happiness and support your mental and emotional state of mind.

Besides diffusing or inhaling essential oils, you can put a few drops on your lava and crystal bracelets, aromatherapy necklaces, in your car and computer plug-ins. Apply a 30% blend (30 drops essential oil to 1 teaspoon carrier oil) to the back of the neck, behind the ears and on the wrists. Putting a drop or two on a sachet of flowers and keeping them near your pillow is very helpful. I bathe in half a cup of Epsom salts and ten drops of any combination of oils. The oils can help to regulate sleep patterns and give you inner peace.

You can try these oils separately or buy them in a blend. Information on getting these oils is on the back page of the book. Below are some of my personal favourites:

1. **Lavender** - is known for its calming and relaxing properties, it can put your nervous system into parasympathetic rest state versus fight or flight. Lavender is a helpful sleep aid.

2. **Frankincense** - The King of oils, is an incredible mood support, helps brain fog, minimizes distractions and improves concentration. It helps with emotional balance and increases spiritual awareness and meditation.

3. **Bergamot** - can help to relieve anxiety, depression, stress and tension. It is uplifting and refreshing. It helps to expand and open the heart chakra and to radiate love energy.

4. **Geranium** - can help to release negative memories and take you back to peaceful, joyful moments. It can ease your nervous tension and stress, balance emotions, lift the spirit, and foster peace, well-being and hope. It can also lower defences that prevent being open and receptive to new beginnings.

5. **Jasmine** - symbolizes hope, happiness, and love. Jasmine affects emotions, penetrating the deepest layers of the soul, opening doors to vulnerability. It can produce a feeling of confidence, energy, and optimism. It can help reduce anxiety, apathy, depression, indifference, and listlessness. It is uplifting to emotions and may help increase intuitive powers and wisdom.

   **Note – one pound of Jasmine Oil requires 1,000 pounds of Jasmine or 3.6 million fresh picked blossoms. Each blossom must be collected by hand before sunrise, or the fragrance evaporates. These properties are based on pure Jasmine essential oil and not synthetic oils.*

6. **Rose (Bulgarian Rose)** - is very helpful in stimulating and elevating the mind to a sense of well-being. Its 320 MHz frequency make it one of the highest energy oils, which enhances the frequency of every cell of the body, bringing it in balance and harmony. Rose can help smooth grief, shock, and help release traumatic emotions associated with grief.

7 **Sandalwood** - Folklore tells us that Sandalwood awakens the latent life force energy during meditation and frees the souls of the deceased. Many cultures still consider this oil to be sacred. In modern times, sandalwood is very similar to FRANKINCENSE in action. It slowly and powerfully calms, harmonizes, and helps balance emotions. It can be stimulating as well as grounding and can fill you with a sense of peace.

8 **Vetiver** - its heavy, smoky and earthy fragrance is psychologically grounding, calming, with stabilizing qualities. It has been valuable for relieving stress and helping people recover from emotional trauma and shock. Known as a natural tranquilizer, it may help induce sleep. It can leave you feeling at peace and grounded.

9 **Ylang Ylang** - helps balance the emotional centres, reduces anxiety, depression, it may help in lowering blood pressure, rapid breathing and anger often associated with loss and grief. It brings back feelings of self-love, healing, confidence, joy and inner peace.

10 **Northern Lights Black Spruce** - was used by the Lakota Indians to enhance their communication with the Great Spirit. Spruce oil creates the symbolic effect of an umbrella that protects the earth and brings energy from the universe. At night the animals in the wild lie down under the trees for protection, recharging, and rejuvenation. Spruce oil grounds the body, creating a feeling of balance to receive and to give. It helps release emotional blocks.

Many oils can help with the grief process, but these are my top ten picks. There is no right or wrong to what works for you. Choose whatever is pleasing to your nose. May they bring you peace, love, and light.

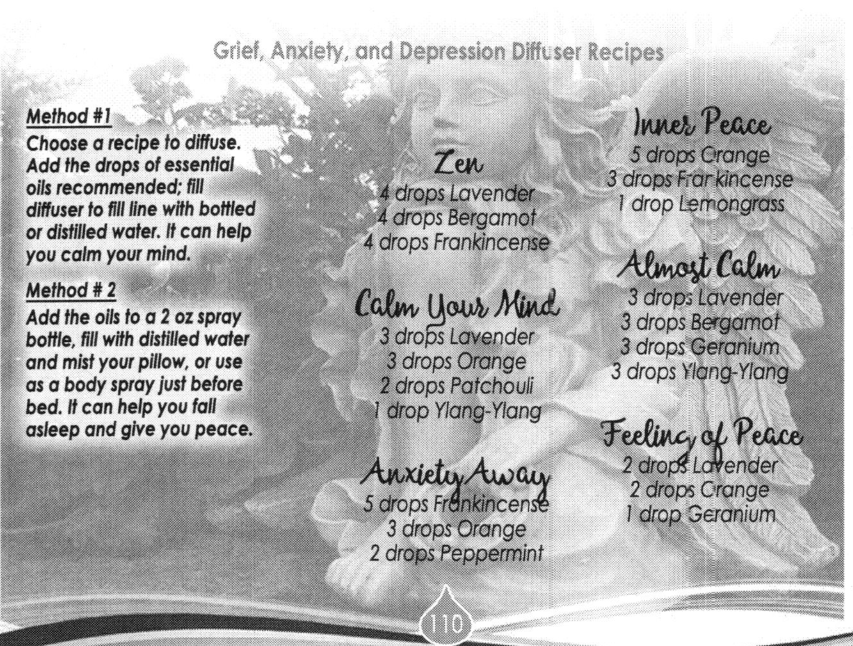

Chapter 16

Bryan's Story

The words "Mom, I have cancer" rocks your world beyond words. Death for us all is inevitable, but when your children face this enemy, it's a battle no mother should have to shoulder, ever! These words devastated me not once, but three times.

December 23, 1996, was when I got the call at work at 4:30 pm that my youngest son's results were in. Dr. Smith at the Hys Medical Centre in Edmonton was on the line. "Do you want the good news or the bad news?" he asked.

My heart half sank as I thought, well it's a 50% chance of something good. "I'll take the 50% bad," I replied. I decided I'd save the good for last.

"The bad news is Bryan's tests came back positive for Hodgkin's Lymphoma; the good news is there is a 96% survival rate," he said. He was brief, to the point. "As a matter of fact, be at the Cross Cancer Institute on January 6." He then asked if I had any other questions, waited for a moment and hung up.

My brain was trying to process this, like okay, he has cancer, but it's treatable? So it's not a big deal? The days before Christmas my gift shop was crazy busy, and the season of celebration was upon us. My baby just turned 18, no real symptoms other than swollen lymph nodes and now was diagnosed with cancer. In those seconds my world flipped upside down. It all seemed like a dream, a bad dream and I had to sit down. The tears came flooding down my cheeks, and my client's haircut would have to wait till I could get a grip on this, clear my blurred vision and process what just took place.

Stage 2-B Hodgkin's Lymphoma, a two-inch tumour in his neck and a four-inch tumour in his lung lining behind his heart. Stage 2-B meant he should have already had all the symptoms, itchy skin, fatigue, and sweats. Other than the very noticeable lump in his neck, Bryan only had fatigue. I can remember him sleeping on Sunday till 1:00 p.m. and wondered how a young guy could sleep the day away. He was always very active, involved in most sports activities: basketball, volleyball, curling, baseball, golf, and many others. He worked with maintenance at the Boyle Golf and Country Club cutting the grass and maintaining the greens (a job he kept while in treatment), he had just graduated grade twelve and volunteered at Shaw Cable one day a week which meant driving two hours one-way to Edmonton. My son was a picture of perfect health, so how could this have even happened?

The doctor thought cancer had been growing for about a year before Bryan felt a lump in his neck, but his active lifestyle and being that he was a bit of a wellness guru, this seemed like a misdiagnosis. I had only hoped it would be that.

Bryan at work and play at Skeleton Lake Golf & Country Club between Treatments.

A cancer diagnosis changes not only the person affected but the entire family. L fe is never and I mean NEVER the same. Bryan went on to battle with chemotherapy, cisplatin and gemcitabine.

Cisplatin was first approved for cancer treatment in 1978, ironically the year Bryan was born. Originally it was created in 1844 by Italian chemist Michele Peyrone. It was known as Peyrone's chloride and is an off-patent, which means no company has exclusive rights and any credible drug company can make it. In 1965, Barnett Rosenberg published his works on this drug with its ability to "cure" cancer. He passed away in 2009, but all royalties from cisplatin provide great benefit to the Michigan State University Foundation (MSU) at cpproximately $450 million a year.

Cisplatin is called the penicillin of cancer because it's so widely used but has dramatic side effects, including nausea, vomiting, low blood counts, kidney toxicity, ototoxicity, low calcium, low potassium, peripheral neuropathy, loss of appetite, taste changes, hair loss, diarrhea, mouth sores, fever with chills, and blood in the urine. Bryan experienced almost all of the above. Cisplatin works by damaging the RNA or DNA that tells the cel how to copy itself in the division. If the cells are unable to divide, they die, causing the tumours to shrink. Unfortunately, chemotherapy does not know the difference between cancerous cells and normal cells, thus causing the side effects. This chemo drug was used alongside gemcitabine but did not work for Bryan as I will explain later.The cancer tumour in his lung lining grew again and he battled a second time.

Three percent of people who take gemcitabine in combination with cisplatin can get cancer of the bone marrow later on in life (I discuss post chemotherapies further down), can cause seizures, abnormal heartbeats, liver damage, shortness of breath, fluid around lungs or scarring of lungs. The less serious side effects are very similar to cisplatin.

Gemcitabine was first discovered in the early 1980s, but the FDA approved it for non-small cell lung cancer in 1998 and approved for metastatic breast cancer in 2004. It is used to treat bladder, pancreas, ovary, breast and non-small cell lung cancers and other cancers as well. Both of these historic drugs did not work eradicating Bryan's Hodgkin's Lymphoma cancer. Both chemo's were also used in Marty's battle with cholangiocarcinoma but did not work.

Six months of this chemotherapy combination, five weeks of daily doses of radiation, and living nearly two hours from the cancer hospital, took its toll physically, mentally, and financially.

Bryan was to begin his Radio and Television Course at NAIT that January 6, 1997, the same day he was scheduled to be at the hospital. He was devastated at the fact he would miss his first day and only agreed to go to the hospital when his dad offered to fill in at school. Together Bryan and I went to the hospital where the typical chemotherapy protocol for Hodgkin's began. He managed to finish his first year at NAIT and by July Bryan was finished his chemotherapy. This did not happen without brutal side effects like neuropathy in his hands and feet, radiation scars, his wisdom teeth had to come out, infection set in, and he was hospitalized two days into writing final exams. The wrenching, headaches, and fatigue were constant as he navigated through school and excelled with marks in the ninety percentiles. Cancer patients go through their battles so courageously and purposefully, persevering with super heroic determination. They all have become my heroes in real life.

Back then holistic medicine was not nearly as researched as it s today and our Master Herbalist, did his best to keep Bryan's immune system at premium levels in spite of the chemicals raising havoc on his body.

Vitamins, tinctures and supplements were his body's only defence system. They were a saving grace where others going through a similar battle were worse off and had to take time off school or their work to get through those horrendous treatments. Despite what oncologists say, our experience was that both boys did far better with holistic-functional science support for their immune systems than they would have without.

By September 1998 he started radiation and that took its toll on an already weakened body. The side effects were equally brutal, especially as time went on. Dry mouth, mouth sores, and swallowing solid foods was painful because the radiation was targeting his lung area where the big tumour was located. This affected his bronchioles, his esophagus and the outer skin both front and back of his chest. It was like he was being microwaved alive. The process was difficult to watch but was what we put our hope in for complete healing. Today Bryan still bears the scars of that five-week torturous endurance marathon.

September was also the beginning of his second and final year at NAIT. His dream of Major League Baseball was taking shape as he was scheduled in October for tryouts with the Atlanta Braves. A scout had invited him to participate in what was an opportunity of a lifetime. Dreams come true. Thinking that with radiation and chemo behind him, Bryan was determined cancer was not going to steal those dreams. As the weeks passed and even though the daily radiation was done, the lasting effects took its toll on his throwing arm and that dream of college baseball would be put on hold, at least for the moment. His compromised immune system became a challenge attending school, but he preserved and went on to graduate with marks in the nineties.

Playing baseball was a passion for Bryan, shown here winning Provincials with the Waskatenau Braves. He played center field.

Soon, another Christmas came and went, and we were all so extremely grateful that the tumours had all shrunk back and it looked like the cancer was eliminated.

1998 was a year to be celebrated for Bryan, with NAIT done and his first television job with CKSA Lloydminster, he was on his way to living his dream of becoming a sportscaster. Bryan was in his element. If baseball was not to be, then this would be the next best. He was settling into a new career and started living his dream.

Bryan's first job was with CKSA Lloydminster, Alberta

By the fall of that year, he developed a cough that would not go away. Busy with his new job, he did not give it much thought till his November regular six-month checkup that was due at the Cross. The CAT scan showed shadows where the four-inch tumour had been. This was not the news we were hoping for. Shadows meant something was going on.

Once again, I got the call, this time from Bryan himself. "Mom my cancer is back."

Like a horror movie that just keeps playing; again we were in battle, seven months had hardly passed since his first three-month clean checkup. Words cannot describe the raw emotions, that become so intrusive on what I call a new sense of normalcy. Clearly, the chemotherapy and radiation did not work. This time the oncologist gave him only a 66% survival rate. Our options were not pretty, and because Bryan had gone through the treatment, he was not looking forward to what lay ahead. Once again dreams shattered as we all tried to pick up the pieces of what we could salvage and make the most of a truly ugly poker hand. We had to win this time. The alternative was not an option.

An avid curler, Bryan qualified with his team to compete in the Provincial Junior Curling Championships in December of '98 that took place in Sundre Alberta. Prior to that, we had to be back at the Cross for pill form chemotherapy, steroids to suppress the immune and a Broviac tube inserted surgically under the skin of his neck through the chest area to the large vein that leads to the heart. That Broviac tube would eventually become the entry to all h s high doses of chemotherapy, bone marrow transplant, and blood transfusions. With the tube inserted, daily chemo, and daily doses of prednisone, all these drugs were suppressing his immune system once again. I was so proud of Bryan for attempting to curl in sp te of his nausea, headaches and fatigue. He would curl a game and immediately head back to the motel to try to sleep it off before the next game. Nothing seemed to come easy, another dream shattered, as we left for home without the win; but more challenging would be the treatment that lay ahead.

Despite being on daily chemo pills, a foot long broviac tube attached to his chest, and chills from the side effects of treatment, Bryan curled his heart out at the Alberta Men's Junior Curling Playoffs.

His team did not win, but Bryan went on to call the game he loved at the Vancouver Olympics, as well as continues to call the Scottie's, The Brier, and World Juniors for TSN.

Nausea, headaches, loss of appetite, and temporary blindness plagued him every day. The scariest is when he called to say he could not see when he awoke one morning. Rushing to his side, I stayed the weekend with him in his Lloydminster condo, leading him around and praying for relief. Unfortunately, an inexperienced doctor he saw was to blame for not recognizing the high fever Bryan had developed. He sent him home instead of contacting his oncologist for further instructions. Several days passed before his sight was restored and we never did find out whether it was a side effect of the drugs the induced fever, or a combination that caused the temporary blindness.

We all looked for a new normal. Normal boring days were welcomed, and to this day I am so grateful for my days that I get to choose my own schedule, enjoy my choices of daily routine, go about my work day, enjoy the simple pleasures of afternoon tea and ice cream if I so desired. It's a privilege that cancer patients and their caregivers are denied. The disease leaves an ugly path of destruction that can take years to overcome.

Survivors are so grateful, take nothing for granted, celebrate their successes, and make every moment in life worth living. Cancer changes you forever.

Somehow, we got through Christmas by going through the motions, but never rearing far from thoughts of what lay ahead. This one was definitely tougher than the previous, because this time we knew somewhat where the battlefield would be. Never then would I have thought 2018, twenty years later would be worse when my older son Marty would endure his battle.

A stem cell transplant is used for hard-to-treat Hodgkin's Lymphoma, especially if it comes back after chemotherapy and radiation. There are two main types of stem cell transplants. The first is autologous stem cell transplant where a patient's own blood stem cells are collected before treatment. They are then frozen and stored while the patient goes through high chemotherapy. This was the procedure that Bryan would endure.The other is an allogeneic stem cell transplant where the blood stem cells come from someone else. This treatment is used only if the autologous transplant is tried without success. Either stem cell transplant is a complex treatment that can cause life-threatening side effects.

After thirty days on the pill chemo and prednisone, it was time to harvest Bryan's own stem cell. I have never witnessed anything so barbaric as this procedure. We went to the Cross Cancer Institute a week before his scheduled hospital stay. Laying on his back, a nurse held one hand as I held his other. The doctor used a special chisel-like instrument that burrowed through his skin and into the marrow of the hipbone. Neither freezing nor anesthesia was given and the pressure that the doctor applied to penetrate that site sent Bryan into agony. He squeezed my hand so tightly I lost circulation in it. My heart stopped, watching him winch in terrible pain. A bit more than a quart of bone marrow and red blood cells was extracted from the site and the procedure took about one hour. The marrow was then filtered to remove fat and particles of bone and frozen for infusion at a later date.

By mid-January 1999, reluctantly taking a leave from his job and me leaving my incredible staff in charge of my gift shop, together, we entered the third-floor isolation wing of the Cross Cancer Institute, which would become home for the next two months. On this floor, there was one nurse for every two patients because the patients' care was critical to their survival.

All hell broke loose within hours of our arrival. Attached to his Broviac tube, the chemicals were poured into that poor child of mine, and I watched helplessly. His fever rose, he hallucinated, and wretched mercilessly, without any letup for thirty-six long hours. Four tough chemo drugs - the aftermath of the side effects of these drugs was beyond anyone's imagination. The side effects would linger on for many more days.

If hell is here on earth, then we were in the midst, fighting for my son's life. We both managed twelve hours of sleep in the ten days that followed. No one could fathom this six-foot one, a 179-pound man would soon weigh 139 pounds. In that dark room, the days melded into nights and nights were oblivious to the day. Every bone hurt, Bryan was bedridden, too weak to lift his head, he lost all body hair, mouth sores made swallowing water painful, bed sores covered his very fragile skin and the light hurt his eyes.

I too became robotic in every move I made. I became a full-time mom nurse, massaging feet, getting the cooling cloths for his very feverish forehead, sponge bathing, and bathroom duties. Eventually, my extremely weak stomach somewhat stopped belching every time my son did, or someone in the room next to us did. Bryan joked about the wrenching that sounded like some way off key symphony trying to work on some new material. Occasional humour in our all-inclusive getaway. I was so uncomfortable with bed and bathroom duties; changing your son's diapers as a baby is one thing, at twenty, it was an entirely different experience.

Once again, my son was diplomatic as always. "Mom," he said, "we got to do what we got to do, just get er done." Yep, we had a job to do here, and this was part of it; my lesson learned.

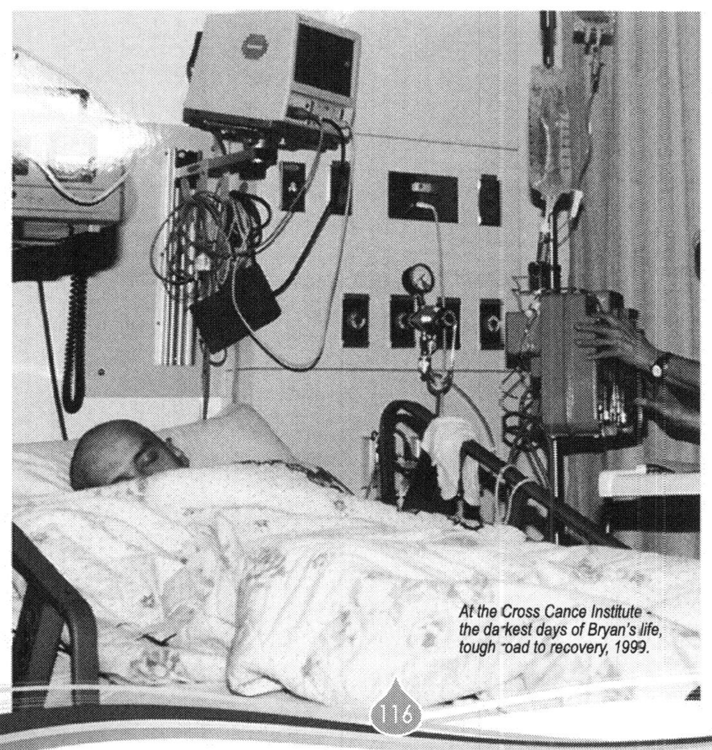

At the Cross Cancer Institute - the darkest days of Bryan's life, tough road to recovery, 1999.

We had no visitors. Visitors could bring in a virus that could kill my son. The risk was far too great. My only contact with the outside world was a newspaper brought by hospital volunteers every other day. I was so grateful for those paper drop-offs just inside our door. My connection to the outside world was through those newspapers, and in spite of the world's own chaos, it seemed dreamy compared to ours.

Soon it was February, and the harvest of Bryan's own stem cells would be relocated back into my son's veins. He joked with the doctor about making sure those harvested stem cells would not be accidentally thrown away. His red blood count was at 100. The normal was from 10,000 - 20,000 range, so his concern was legitimate; without that infusion of his harvested stem cells, he would die. The chemo drugs killed every bit of his immune system, and this was his only chance of survival. We were about one-third of the way through this horrible battle.

One night we nearly lost him, and I remember getting down on my knees and praying to God, pleading to save my son even though I knew he could take him. I gave him to God that day, and it felt like I stood on the edge of a high mountain cliff and leaped in faith only God could save my son. As mothers, we protect and love our children. We would leap off a mountain cliff if it meant saving them; that was my most helpless moment and although at the time I felt free, nineteen years later, that helplessness would return to haunt me again. As I write this the tears seem to find their way down my cheeks and cloud my vision.

Cancer sucks!

The transplant started at 11:00 a.m. and took about four hours before all quarts of bone marrow mixture was infused through his Broviac tube. The mix was held on ice and each bag was liquid crystals, not frozen, but not fully thawed, so when it entered Bryan's heart through the tube and began spreading throughout his veins, his body went into freeze mode. He became so cold, nothing could warm him, and he shivered uncontrollably.

Recovery in the following weeks was painfully slow; every day Bryan's blood was tested to see if the stem cell count was going up. The second day was no show, the third day it went to 200, the fourth 400, the fifth day it stayed the same, and that was scary considering normal was 20,000. We had a long way to go.

Bryan agreed to try a trial drug that would help increase the levels quicker. Soon his fever spiked and every night by 11:00 pm the headache and sweats were unbearable. Sleep was not happening in that dark and dreary room during the month of March. This continued on for a week when they thought perhaps he had contracted a liver infection that would mean another month stay in the hospital. I mentioned to one of his favourite nurses that the fever seemed to spike at night and release by morning, so something was definitely causing this out of the ordinary symptom. She decided it was the trial drug and when it was discontinued the fevers stopped and of course the liver tests came back negative.

We could receive few family and friend visitors and that helped break the isolation we were immersed in for so long.

Soon the blood counts were rebounding in double and triple digits, and the light of coming home was in the near future. We were mid-March and Bryan was looking forward to his invitation as guest speaker for the 1999 graduation class in Boyle. Still bedridden with the event six weeks away, it looked like that would be one more missed event. But we still had time and he was optimistic.

Leaving the hospital in a wheelchair, my frail son asked to pause a moment as we got to the foyer of the hospital. Wrapped in a blanket and wearing a toque over his bald head, he looked back at the hospital and said, "Mom, one day we will raise a million dollars for this hospital."

I must admit - in my exhaustion of what we had just endured I just shook my head yes, all the while wondering how that would ever come to be.

Coming home was a celebration. Still requiring bed rest, I set up a temporary bedroom for Bryan in the living room and his Baba would babysit him on the days I went to work. Financially with all costs associated with the three-year battle was $25,000.00; that included holistic medicine, medication not covered by our health plans and the cost of parking, food, lodging and covering Bryan's expenses while he was unable to work.

Slowly week by week he became stronger and although was still very fragile, he did speak to a full house at the graduation ceremonies, where he got a standing ovation.

Only 7 weeks after leaving the Cross Cancer Institute after his intense Bone marrow transplant, Bryan kept his speaking engagement in front of a full Boyle School Auditorium at their 1999 Graduation ceremonies. His motivational speech made a lasting impact on those graduates. He received a standing ovation.

Robby Williams and Marty Mudryk spearheaded the Williams & Mudryk 100 K, and alongside Bryan's Angels, Bryan, I with family and friends, raised 1.8 million dollars for equipment at the Cross Cancer Institute and over $120,000 to Knight's Cabin to help cancer patients embrace wellness after diagnosis; that is another story. Check our website www.MuddyPhilanthropy.ca for more information.

2016 event: Bryan and many of the volunteers that helped make the Bryan Mudryk Golf Calssic such a huge success.

Fifteen years later, with Marty, Robby Williams, and Bryan

Front row: Terry and Bryan Mudryk, Ian Frank. Back row: Bryan's Angels who came on board and helped make the $1.8 million a reality.

Today Bryan is living his dream at TSN, calling play-by-play NHL Hockey for the Montreal Canadiens, and play-by-play curling for Scotties, Brier, and World Junior Curling.

Cancer patients who have endured the battle, have a bigger challenge of making sure that their cancer does not return. Bryan, now years later, continues to be proactive so that the damage that was inflicted on his DNA during his three years of radical chemo and radiation treatments is no longer a deterrent to his health. He has eliminated sugar, white flour, processed foods, and pork.

He has a huge supplement protocol, drinks Ningxia wolfberry every single day, and diffuses essential oils as well as topical applications, exercises and lives chemical free in his personal space. He is on a diet consisting of organic fruit and vegetables, grass-fed meats, and wild ocean fish. Bryan has taken testing at Neurvanna Health to determine what damage was done and where his body is struggling to keep his immune optimum. He has undergone testing for toxicity, stool testing to look for stressors on the immune system and issues with nutrient absorption, organic acid testing to look at detoxification, energy production, stress, nutrient deficiencies, and comprehensive hormone and peptide evaluation to be sure his immune system is regulating properly.

It's no secret that the state of our health, as well as health care, is becoming chronic and in dire straits. Today we live in a world in which we are constantly bombarding our bodies with dangerous and often deadly toxins. We eat highly processed fake foods and drink chemically infused water (fluoride, lead and VOC'S). We continue to believe those headaches, tummy aches, and body inflammation will go away, or we pop pharmaceuticals, which contribute to bigger gut issues.

Health is wealth — if you think wellness is expensive, try illness. Our family urges you to make changes now: change your diet, exercise, feed your soul, meditate, volunteer, and give back to your community, reduce stress by massage, reading, diffusing essential oils, and keeping positive vibes. Investing in yourself now will save you money – a whole lot of money for many years to come. Choose wellness.

Bryan's
growing-up days.
He loved baseball,
golf, hockey,
the lake life,
and Garfield.

Chapter 17

Marty's Journey

I love everyday normal days; normal and uneventful days are my favourite. Some might call them boring, but this mom totally enjoys those nothing rocking your boat, all is well, life is good, kind of days....

That is until on May 3, 2017, I get a call from my firstborn son, "Where are you, mom?"

"At work," I replied.

He was brief. "I will call you later at home."

I should have picked up on the fear in his voice, but work distractions took those thoughts and set them aside. I left work a bit earlier that day, and the moment I walked through the door, the phone was ringing. It was Marty.

The words that haunted me some twenty years earlier, echoed in my ears once more. "Mom, I have cancer and a really bad kind. The doctor said it's very aggressive and stage four."

My heart stopped beating momentarily; I felt like I stopped breathing as I tried to grasp the three words I had heard twice before in 1996 – 99, "I have cancer," from my youngest son Bryan. Life sometimes is just not fair. I listened to my eldest son explain his options, which were really none.

"Get your affairs in order," the doctor told him, "you have cholangiocarcinoma."

I burst into uncontrollable sobs. Not my first born too. So many thoughts raced through my head all at once, as I tried to regroup my thoughts moving forward. I gave birth to this child of mine, and I knew whatever it took, I would give him a fighting chance, and more than the doctors promised and more than his forty-three years that he had just celebrated less than two weeks prior. I promised him I would leave no stone unturned and whatever the universe had out there, we would uncover, and the three months he was given, we would work together to make him an outlier.

He jumped on board and what a journey that became. We both felt like pioneers in the early days breaking new ground and testing new territory. Functional Science Research and holistic modalities became our best friends.

Marty's symptoms came suddenly as all liver, gallbladder, pancreatic and bile cancers do. On Friday he ran five kilometres, lifted weights for half an hour. Saturday, he felt like he had food poisoning, perhaps from the hamburger he ate at the arena while watching Teegan play hockey. That feeling did not go away, and by Sunday his urine was a dark brown, his eyes were yellow, his skin became extremely itchy and by Tuesday he was in the hospital having a surgical stent implanted in his bile duct. Without the surgery, he would die.

Cancer blocked the duct that carries bile from the liver to the first part of the small intestine and is not detected until symptoms appear. By then it's generally stage IV (4) cancer.

The cancer started in the cells of the inner lining of the bile duct. This was our welcome to the world of cholangiocarcinoma stage IV, which meant it had spread. In Marty's case, the cancer had metastasized into the liver and the lungs. In later stages, it would spread into the intestinal wall.

Although he was moved immediately to palliative care, Marty left the hospital less than a week after diagnosis. The Saturday night prior I had called Corey Deacon, a neuroscientist with a doctorate in natural medicine, a board certified holistic alternative medicine practitioner, and a friend with whom I previously worked alongside in client referrals. He immediately saw Marty for the start of many functional science tests and had them sent state-side for analyzing and diagnosis.

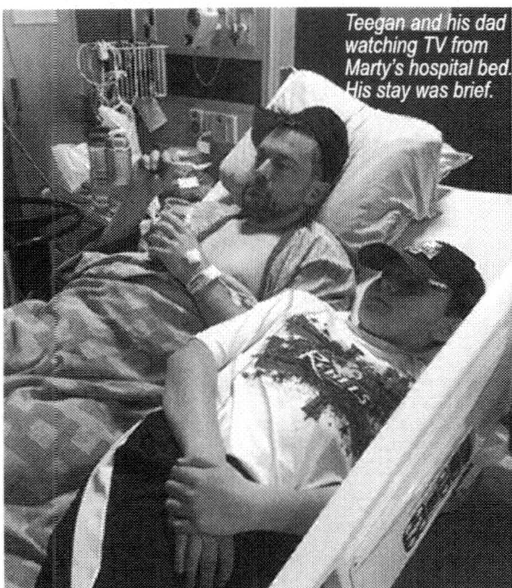

Despite resistance from Marty's oncologist who gave him no hope, he chose to implement every modality available to him. Eventually, he would say when he spoke at wellness seminars, "When you cannot give me Hope, then do not steal that Hope which is mine." With that, he went on to beat three timelines the doctors gave him.

This is Marty's journey, shared through his mother's love and faith that would not give up hope for her son. Good times, fun times, tough and difficult times, praying through the pain and finding peace in the journey.

The Cross Cancer Institute was second on the list of possible healing options. The oncologist offered two chemo combinations which included gemcitabine and cisplatin. I questioned her on this as it was the same combination Bryan was on twenty years earlier in 1996 for Hodgkin's Lymphoma. Her answer was it was the best that they had available.

Gemcitabine also is known as Gemzar and was discovered by scientists at the pharmaceutical company Eli Lily and the Food and Drug Administration (FDA) approved it in 1998. FDA warnings include pulmonary toxicity, respiratory failure, bladder toxicity, liver damage, plus a host of other nasty side effects like fever, chills, muscle and joint aches, and lowered platelet counts.

Cisplatin has a longer history as it was first created by Italian chemist Michele Peyrone in 1844, known as Peyrone's Chloride. In an accidental experiment by Dr. Barnett Rosenberg in 1965, he discovered platinum compounds released affected cell division dramatically. In spite of the idea of putting heavy metals into humans, based on positive results, the National Cancer Institute (NCI) began funding clinical trials of cisplatin in human cancer patients. Successful results in advanced testicular cancer led to the FDA approval of cisplatin in 1978 for testicular, ovarian, and bladder cancer.

According to the NCI, the death rate from testicular cancer has dropped two-thirds since 1975. Unfortunately, researchers are still trying to figure out why it does not work for all patients.

Cisplatin's long term side effects can cause hearing loss and tinnitus, which is a ringing in the ears and neuropathy which causes weakness, numbness, and pain in the hands and feet. Twenty years later after his battle, Bryan struggles with tinnitus and uses supplements and essential oils to help repair the damage done by the multiple doses of chemotherapy he received.

Despite no evidence that these chemo drugs would be helpful, Marty chose to do six months of treatments. He started in May 2017 and finished one week on, two weeks off in October of that year.

Soon after the release of his one week stay in the hospital after his initial surgery, Marty started a very strict sugar-free diet, based on Keto. He became a protégé patient, very committed, extremely rigid in his functional health protocol, and very open to all natural health options. I discussed many of them in detail in previous chapters in this book. Options included Reiki energy healing, body talk, floating salt baths, high dosages of intravenous vitamin C and vitamin D, infrared sauna therapy, raindrop massage therapy, crystal healing therapy, meditation, acupuncture, exercise, Young Living essential oils both topically and internally, Ningxia wolfberry, curcumin IV, Blackseed oil, Vitamin B17, mistletoe injections, and more than thirty different supplements and vitamins that he took three times a day which amounted to about forty pills per serving, the equivalent of 130 or more per day. He also removed pork completely from his diet.

My son battled hard, and he worked hard to do all he could to get the most of what life had to offer him. Tears flowed many times as I researched options, contacted every doctor I knew who might have new information, and watched my son fight for his life like a soldier at war, but at least a soldier had a better chance of survival than anyone battling terminal cancer.

A song that Marty often referred to and I think is extremely fitting for all cancer patients, is a song by Hail Storm called the "Black Vultures." The words go something like this:

> *I'm on the edge of the war, I'm holding on and hanging by a thread.*
> *I am the eye of the storm, and you haven't seen the last of me just yet.*
> *I have fallen down but I'm not out, I'm coming back for more.*
> *I don't give in, I don't give up. I won't ever let it break me.*
> *I'm on fire, I'm a fighter. I'll forever be the last one standing....*

No one can relate more to this song than a cancer patient fighting for her or his life.

The blessings of all of the supplements, all the therapies, and all of Marty's diligence was that three months into the battle when doctors said he would be gone, he excelled. He was back at work within a couple of weeks of his surgery, he was working out at the gym, and he told me he felt and looked the best he ever had been. He took his family on a summer vacation in 2017 to see the Seattle Mariners, and besides his work at Enbridge, he focused on both of his sons' hectic hockey schedules.

Marty and his boys loved the game. Both on Skeleton Lake, in the local arenas or watching the beloved Oilers and Oil Kings. They were season tickets holders to both teams in typical Canadian passion and heart, "He shoots – he scores!"

A CAT Scan in November showed remarkable shrinkage and the doctors were surprised at his gradual improvement. Christmas 2017 had great memories of ice fishing and playing hockey on North Skeleton Lake with family and friends. I cooked an organic grass fed turkey with all the trimmings, the annual skating rink was abuzz with fun and laughter and indeed family time was precious.

January 2018 CAT Scan once again showed more shrinkage much to all of our delight. He was four months on natural therapies only. Western medicine had nothing more to offer at this time. During this period Marty had many tests done such as DHA-metabolic panel DHA-SAME/SAH methylation profile, DHA Organix Comprehensive profile, Cyrex-Array 2-3-11-12, Labrix-NeuroHormone Complete, MVL-CSDA, MVL-UrineMinerals 6, MVL-Kraft-(bloodspot), MVL Essential Fatty Acids, MVL-Plasma Amino Acids, QEEG Brain Mapping and Neurocognitive Assessment, Bio health, SIBO breath test, BHL-Bile Acids, and MVL-IGFI tests. Because both my sons battled cancer, Marty and Bryan were also tested for DNA Genetics, but both proved negative. Through this extensive testing, we did find the causes of both boys' cancer was enviro-chemical.

The bacteria, environmental, chemical, moulds and toxins compounded with grief when he lost his infant daughter five years previous, were all contributors to Marty's cancer. As the tests came back, testing positive, those were the first issues that were addressed. Marty became chemical free in 24/7. Dryer sheets were replaced with wool balls, laundry soap, personal toiletries, (all replaced with Young Living Thieves Cleaning line). Marty's wife Kristen became excellent at finding healthier recipes, cooking up some amazing dinners as cleaner eating, exercise, and overall wellness therapies became the new normal. This became a permanent lifestyle change, not just for himself, but he led the way for greater awareness of well- being, and being pro-active was shared to extended family, including his brother. Those changes have made his legacy live on in each of us, and he hoped that message would go far and wide!

If you think wellness is expensive, try Illness – he encouraged everyone to make changes before the chronic disease takes hold.

Scientists have found Helicobacter Pylori, a bacterium usually found in the stomach can increase the risk of stomach cancer. The research findings which they report in a study published in the "PLOS ONE Journal" may change the way in which specialists screen for and treat this type of cancer.

Some of the hottest contemporary research, concerns the role of bacteria in cancer and cancer treatments. Dr. Michael Karin, a professor of molecular biology at the UC San Diego School of Medicine and winner of the Coley Award, has helped draw attention to the link between bacteria and cancer. "Inflammation is believed to account for about 20% of all cancers, but probably plays a role in more than 80 to 90% of all cancers," says Karin.

Studies at the Harvard School of Public Health show a strain of bacteria called fusobacterium nucleatum are found prevalent in colorectal cancer patients. More information can be found at www.cancerresearch.org.

At the beginning of April, I received an email from Marty. The March CAT Scan showed slight positive movement from the tumours and that was concerning. We were still getting much resistance from Marty's oncologist as to our own research and possible protocol changes. I believe our battle integrating functional science health with conventional medicine was far greater than the cancer battle itself. At this time Marty's original biopsy was requested to be sent to a lab in Houston, Texas where his DNA and the cancer cells could be grown to see what possible treatments would be helpful in shrinking his tumours. The cancer hospital agreed to send it off and we would patiently wait the two months for a possible new direction with more options.

Another email from Marty came April 11, 2018 and was a quick update to Corey and me. This is what it read:

> #1. I incorporated olive oil starting yesterday morning, puked on the side of the road on the way to work. Haven't done that in some time. Back then it was not olive oil induced! Will have to try different ways to incorporate today with hopefully less excitement.
>
> ***(There was always humour in everything that Marty did and said, and I guess that's what will keep us always smiling when we think about the many little pranks that he pulled on probably more people than we know.)*
>
> #2. Had the bellybutton checked out. Ultrasound is being set up as some sort of moveable sensitive mass was felt by the doctor. Stay tuned.
>
> #3. Spoke to Dr. Denault. He will be contacting you regarding the curcumin. A little bit concerned about the dose, but also provided a good review on Avastin. His pharmacy background will be very beneficial to our team. He did a blood test on me prior to vitamin C IV to ensure I was a suitable candidate.
>
> #4. Could not for the life of me get a hold of my oncologist yesterday despite leaving messages. I did get a hold of her technician and left the following message with direction. Looking at incorporating Avastin into my protocols based on recent blood test results I'm looking to hear her thoughts. Still looking for my May 2017 biopsy to see if we could send it to the lab for more consideration if not, I would like to schedule another one. And lastly, I put in a request for a PET Scan. Further to this, I instructed her somewhat sternly that you and Corey are a part of our team regarding planning the next steps for me and need to be included in this process. I reminded her that you have complete access to all my medical files including what happens at their facility. My direction was that if she had any concerns with the request above to contact you directly so a conversation can take place and we can come up with the best course of action. I am hoping this brings everyone together, working together for one common cause. But that remains to be seen.

This email outlined Marty's concerns with the medical system, and lack of direction for him going forward. His favourite saying once again, "Upwards and onwards," took precedence, because a month had gone by and we still had no direction. He found a book which was one of his favourites called Radical Remission by Dr. Kelly B. Turner. Marty found comfort in reading the book, in that his battle with stage IV metastasized cancer, was not his alone.

Spring was in the air, Marty had his 44th birthday on April 21, and he felt for the first time a slip in his well-being. We had Plan B if needed, and after much research decided to go to Tijuana to see Dr.Isai Castillo Ramos. We had also heard many positive stories coming from his clinic as not much was happening on the home front. One month later on May 21, 2018, we arrived in Tijuana.

Marty was tired and the flight had caused some ascites. Earlier in the month he had some ascites activity in the lung area and had to have it drained, but now his feet became very bothered by it. The most common cause of ascites is an advanced liver disease and can be treated with liquid drains and replacing lost protein with 50 ml. of albumin. The long flight had in some ways aggravated the situation.

The days of the first week quickly became a blur as we try to find our new life. The first week was busy, getting tests done, a protocol in place and addressing Marty's bigger issue of ascites that settled into his feet, legs, and abdomen. Dr. Espinoza encouraged Marty to get a permanent catheter. The draining aids in cancer cell reduction, and helps the therapies become more productive, he said.

The very next day, we met with a top-notch surgeon at Angelo Hospital, Dr. Jorge Zavala. With a mild sedative and a local anesthetic, a 2-inch incision was made in Marty's abdomen. The 35-minute procedure installed the drain tube and drained about six litres of fluid from the area. Marty had relief, the pressure subsided, and this would become the site of daily one litre extractions. The hospital stay was brief, and a CAT Scan ruled out any possible blockages, which was a relief to both patient and this mama. Marty's blood work remained excellent, and I have to attest that due to the 6 to 8 ounces of Ningxia Wolfberry that he drank every day. The procedure, the CAT Scan and the surgery cost $3,500 US. That had to be paid upfront.

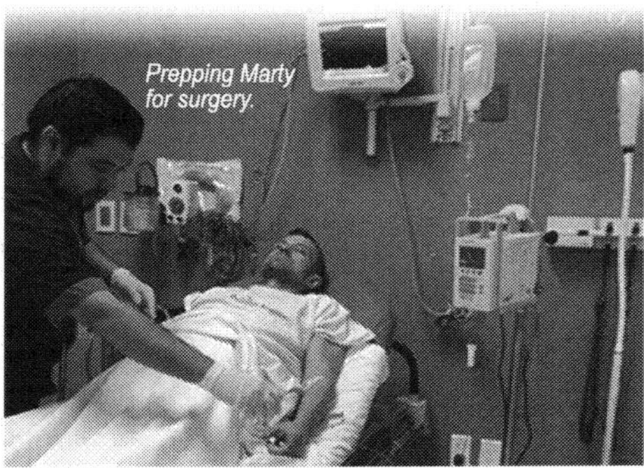

We went back to the clinic for daily IVs which included eight ounces of mixed vitamins, 50 ML of vitamin B-17, eight ounces of DMSO and 50 ML of Albumina Humana Grifols.

Marty's diet would change from Keto to a Hoxsey diet alongside a chemo regime. There was so much to absorb in that first week that we arrived and enduring the surgery was no easy feat. That in itself was very emotional, and being able to see two of Marty's doctors, his surgeon and his oncologist in one afternon, (all arranged that noon) is beyond fantastic service. But that's the Mexico I love, one of the best medical systems in the world.

Back in our hotel, Marty's back pain was unbearable. The 13-hour flight took its toll. The relaxants the doctors gave him seemed to no longer work. All I had was essential oils. I lathered him every three hours throughout the night. My pain recipe appeared to take the edge off, and we both managed to get some sleep. It always brings tears to my eyes knowing how hard he battled and how much pain he endured in the process of trying to get better. Marty, like all cancer patients, will forever be my heroes. We got through the first week adjusting to our new life and trying to get some protocol in place that would become the norm going forward.

Every day is new, every day is something different. As creatures of habit we are waiting for a new normal to start happening - some sort of routine so we know what to expect, and of course the unexpected is always a challenge.

Manny, our cab driver, picked us up at the Rosarito Hotel every morning at 7 a.m. He was assigned to us by the Cipag Clinic as our personal cab driver and was one of the most helpful guys who did so much over and above to make our stay a pleasant one.

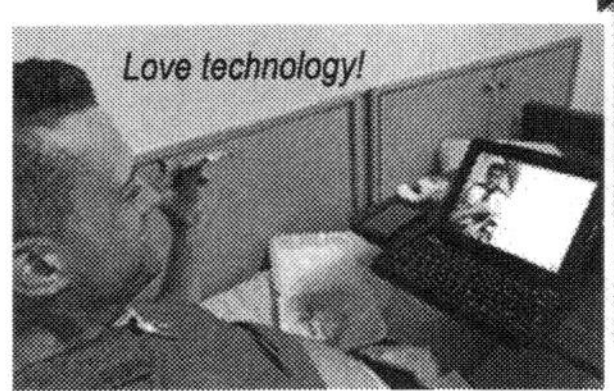

So enjoying the time with my son. Although the journey is difficult, I am so grateful to be able to help him through it.

Marty has not had sugar in over a year, starving cancer.

Back at the clinic, we were introduced to the Hoxsey Diet and chemotherapy program, which is very different from what we know it to be. This is where immediately after the chemo treatment, the patient is encouraged to eat lots of sugar for one hour. In theory, this opens up the cancer cells that feed on the glucose to also infuse the chemo at the same time. Fascinating concept. Nevertheless, it was pure joy to see Marty thoroughly enjoy the Dairy Queen blizzard and four ice-cream cookie bars. This became our weekly stop every Thursday and this was our little bit of heaven in the weeks that followed. It made chemo treatments bearable knowing treats were awaiting afterward.

Most nights, Marty's cramping calves and ankles brutally awakened us. I was so grateful for Cool Azul, Valor essential oil, and my pain massage recipe. Applying and massaging had him back sleeping like a baby in no time, except for me wide-awake from the horrible scream that startled my deep sleep. But sleep did come, and when morning came, the day greeted us with a repeat of daily routine. The high dosages of vitamins, DMSO, vitamin B-17, and then glutathione was added to the protocol, all done by IV.

Marty giving himself his B17 shots.

Marty was shown how to inject his own vitamin 317, and soon he became a pro at it. The Hoxsey Diet is more lenient than the Keto Diet. It includes a special organic whole wheat flour that is GMO-free, easier to digest, with no side effects of gut disruption. His favourite lunch special was an organic chicken veggie Hoxsey pizza with pineapple and watermelon on the side. He also drank a Hoxsey cancer juice packed with one medium-sized beet, two medium carrots, two sticks of celery, 1/8 purple onion, one large garlic clove, half an orange pepper, half a yellow pepper, and three radishes blended with eight ounces of water. It was a great way to get the daily veggie intake done.

We usually got back to our hotel room by about 4 or 5 pm. Our room was basic, with two double beds, and it was clean and comfortable. I set up a makeshift kitchen with an old, dilapidated table we borrowed, a small fridge and toaster that we purchased, and our laundry was done in the bathtub and hung on the balcony to dry. This was our home sweet home for the coming month, and we settled into it nicely.

By the beginning of week three, things got easier in some areas of Marty's health, we saw improvements in his ascites, but just when something gave him relief, something else would become an issue. One morning was particularly tough. Our cabbie waited nearly an hour as Marty tried to get himself comfortable enough for the ride. The muscle relaxant for his back muscles put his bowels in sleep mode and caused constipation that landed us back into the emergency. The doctor decided that we should be kept in for observation and so we settled in for the night. A CAT Scan ruled out any possible blockages. Marty's blood work remained excellent, and with a little bit of help, his bowel movements became regular. He was served organic chicken and organic vegetables for dinner. The food was excellent and incredibly fresh for every meal.

The hospital was a modern up-to-date facility with a full bath, shower and towels. Much to our surprise, personal toiletries were supplied. The technology and equipment was state of the art. The hospital room there was very comfortable, and as Dr. Espinosa said, "It's a high-end hotel with healing powers." Nothing that $3,500.00 US would not cover for our three-day stay.

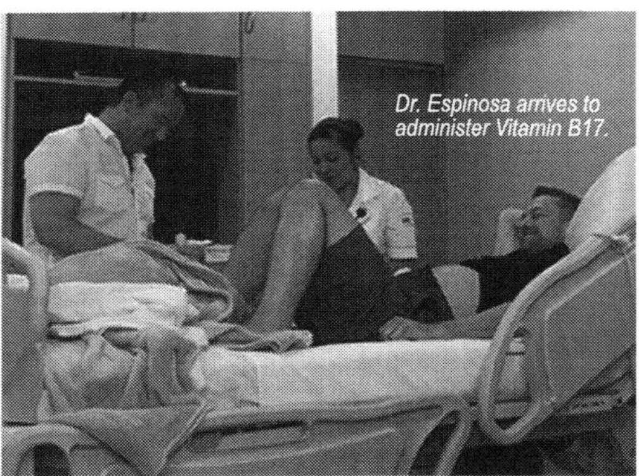

Technology kept Marty in touch with the home front and his family. Hooking up to watch his boys Teegan and Jesse play hockey and connect through videos and text messages always brought smiles to his face.

The cold weather in Tijuana took me by surprise, as May and June were very cold. That sent me shopping for long sleeve sweaters and leggings. Marty had brought a couple of sweaters, so I kept the laundry tub busy every other day re-washing our meager wardrobe. The temperatures were always below 15° Celsius during the day and 4 to 5° during the evening with cold winds. The locals brought tents and parkas when they would hang out at the beach. No two days were identical but at least we were settling into our new home and the routine.

Chilling out, grounding and reflecting on another day. So grateful for every one of them.

At the clinic, we met many patients from Sandy Beach, Sherwood Park, St. Paul, Stony Plain, Elk Point, and a Hutterite family from Two Hills colony. Having so many people there from Alberta made us feel like we were at home. Many also came from British Columbia, Saskatchewan, and Ontario, Canada as well as the Amish and Mennonite families from the United States.

Prostate, lung, bladder, brain, breast, and bone, cancers were most prevalent, and all of them were in either stage three or four. These people come here for hope, hope that our system back home no longer gives them. Every day some leave and more come. Some are repeats, and others come for the first time. Unfortunately, not everyone makes it, but many come because our systems gave up on them. Many get an extension of life that was not available at home. The stories are all the same, but different people telling them. This clinic and all of its amazing staff can add time to a life, so it is an incredibly powerful place of hope and healing.

Considering his battle, Marty set a huge short term goal to make it back to San Diego for a Padres versus Red Sox baseball game. He said it would be my delayed Mother's Day and birthday combined. Very fitting, he said for his baseball mama who drove her boys all summer long to baseball games across Alberta. This would be the first professional baseball game that I would attend, and I was super excited as was Marty. That memory will be my forever favourite of my son. We must grasp those moments that we get when we can, because we can. Marty was such a planner and had everything looked after in spite of his struggles. It meant lining up two cab drivers, one to take us to the border and one who had a passport to take us across the US border. The lineups were insane, with 26 cross terminals and (currently building eight more). Every line was backed up for hours. Patients who stayed stateside, crossed this border every day to the clinic. Most days they had a 3 to 4-hour wait, especially going home. We were grateful we chose to stay in Rosarito. On top of the daily grind, this would be exhausting in itself.

We got past the border and in spite of Marty's tough week of surgery, his hospital stay, his very swollen feet, he let nothing get in the way of that game. We walked a lot, enjoyed a bright sunny warm day, which was one of few and enjoyed the entire day. The Padres won with a grand slam. The facility was incredible, and I was in awe of the vastness of that stadium. Sharing this experience with Marty will forever be etched in my heart. Unfortunately, he paid the price, and he hurt everywhere so with an oil rub-down and his feet elevated, a book in hand, he enjoyed a deserved much-needed rest.

The San Diego Park.

Being so far from home, you rely on God during alone times, when your mind wants to run wild, the severe emotional times when your world is crying in front of you, the physical journey that is filled with pain and suffering, and the days that go by quickly and yet so slowly.

Finally going into the beginning of week four, Marty gets some relief from the ascites. His feet are normal, his ankles and toes are normal for the first time in forever. Two days in a row, we saw progress, and we both cried with emotion and gratefulness. So grateful for these doctors who perservered even when things looked grim.

Sitting poolside in the gardens on a sunny afternoon.

Another consultation with Dr. Espinosa gave us the raw truth in discussions on Marty's arrival to this clinic. We found out the doctors were going to send him home, he was a tough case, and they were not certain that they could help him. But Dr. Espinosa said his gut told him that he had to try and so that was the beginning of our journey here in Tijuana. It's an emotional roller coaster realizing that a decision of one human can cost a life of another and definitely heart-stopping to think that the medical system can determine your fate with the single decision. We had gone through so much that I will never trust or let a system be the judge of my life or my family's life. We all need to research and except nothing less than what you believe to be the best. We were so thankful to Dr. Espinosa and his decision going forward. This week Marty's tests were so positive, that really put a smile on the doctor's face and tears in Marty's eyes. It was overwhelming for him. The doctors back home gave him a timeline twice, but looking back at our journey, Marty's journey, that in itself was sheer suicide. A weak mind would have given up. This was the best Marty felt in a long while and now going home for Father's Day was going to be his next goal. He was elated.

Being regimental is a strict process, and I will always admire Marty for his stamina, endurance, and perseverance in taking his massive protocol of vitamins, supplements, essential oils and therapies. He courageously and without complaining, swallowed over 130 different supplements every single day.

Marty has his feet up after therapies.

Marty's stash of supplements.

Therapies remained the same, repeated day after day, week after week, with chemo on Thursdays. When in a battle, no two days are alike, no two nights the same, and the pain and suffering are constant in some facet for cancer patients. Why one day or night changes, is always the question. More importantly, it is how to fix and how to make it easier for the patient. God becomes your guide.

The cold weather and the chemo took its toll and Marty came down with a cough, flu-like symptoms and a bit of fever one week before leaving for home. His laboured breathing was scary and during the night, we decided to do a litre drain to ease some pressure off his lungs. I rubbed his chest and back into thieves essential oil mix. Very soon, his cough subsided, and he slept well through the night. It's always about figuring out how to manage the situation best when issues arise.

Marty was always so giving and that giving heart never stopped when he was in Tijuana. Even through his pain and difficulty breathing, he went shopping for a bunch of school supplies and socks for kids with HIV that lived in an orphanage in Tijuana. He also financially supported his two nurses who were walking 5 km to help pay for kids' cancer therapies.

Marty and his two sweetheart nurses who were walking five kilometres for kids with cancer.

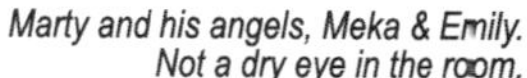

Marty and his angels, Meka & Emily. Not a dry eye in the room.

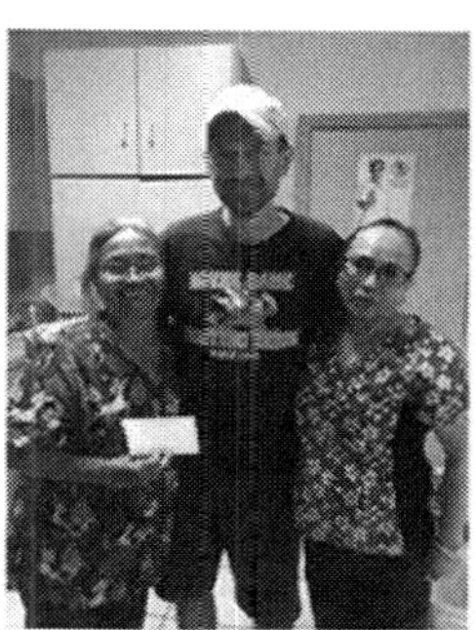

There was always so much good in every day, and we were grateful for those moments.

The doctors concentrated on getting Marty's infection under control with an antibiotic injection. They gave him a second one that he would have to inject himself that evening. This was something that he thought I could do, but my stomach went into spasms just thinking about it. Where is my RN sister when I need her? So together deep breathing, teamwork and "get er done", we did it.

Grateful for small victories his cough subsided, his feet and ankles continue to improve and pretty much stayed normal. We had our last Sunday as a nothing sort of day. We went out shopping, we did a bit of walking along the beach, and a bit of relaxing. Life was the best it had been in some time.

The unexpected became somewhat of a normal. A few more days of therapies and then his drain site became infected. Everyday challenges made the spirit grow weary. I made a thieves spray and applied it to the area. I carefully cleaned and re-dressed the site. Thankfully by morning, the redness was gone. Amazing, but not surprising, the oils worked their magic one more time. I left the mix with the nurses because they were so pleased with the results.

The doctors there worked side-by-side with Marty's doctor of Natural Health Corey Deacon back in Alberta. It was incredible teamwork with functional science and Western medicine combined. Besides all the supplements Marty was on Dr. Castillo put him on 10 grams of Vitamin C (2 tablespoons) and said all cancer patients should be on high dosages of vitamin C.

Just a few days before leaving for home, Marty's drain site sprung a leak. By the time we got to the clinic, the drain had soaked Marty's clothes. Clearly, it had to be re-stitched. The specialist was not able to get to the clinic until the next day, so armed with maxi-pads (yes, maxi-pads!) and gauze pads he persevered that night. Not fancy but it worked. This definitely caused us some worry because, with only a few days left before going home, we both knew he had to be stable to fly. Postponing would mean Marty would not be home to be with his family for Father's Day, and that made us both sad.

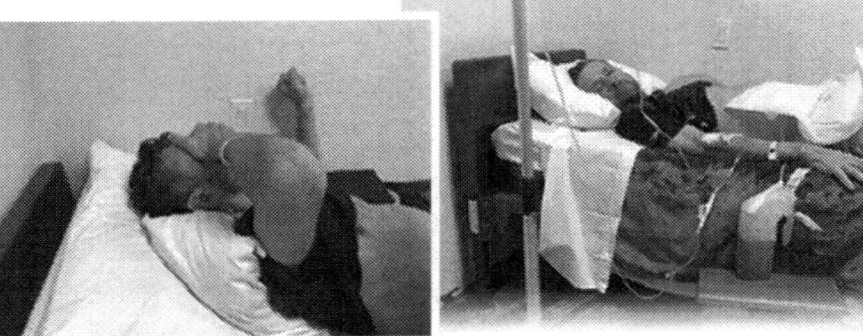

The pain is excruciating while his site dressing is changed. So much pain this month.

The mini surgery was done and once again gave him pain where it had been stitched. The leak was stopped. Packing up all his supplements, oils and our belongings made for a bittersweet goodbye. In spite of the fact he hurt from the eight stitches to the belly, he said, "Boy, I wish this was my first day feeling like I do today going forward." The doctors were impressed with his progress and were very encouraging.

It was almost surreal...this hotel had been our home for a month. The ride each day to the clinic, the therapies, the pain and suffering, the many blessings, so many awesome people we had met and became friends, the fantastic doctors and nurses that cared so much about Marty, all this that made going home feel so foreign. We knew too well the reality of all the hoops we need to jump to get this kind of care at home in just one small clinic like here in Tijuana. But home is where the heart is and we missed our families and our friends.

Home sweet home Tijuana. Marty and I will always love you.

He planned to come back in three weeks, and he proceeded to book flights and accommodations. Unfortunately, that never came to be.

We had been home for just over two weeks. It was a whirlwind of trying to keep Marty stabilized since returning from Tijuana. Unfortunately, our health system nowhere compares to that system and it was a struggle to find someone who could administer albumin, do a drain, and blood work/IV all in one place. Our health care has home care but not the kind of care Marty needed.

The clinic on the south side of Edmonton, Optimum Health, had been giving him his vitamin C and glutathione IV. Marty had to push his own vitamin B17 as that is illegal in Canada.

After a week, his family doctor did find a clinic in St. Albert that would give him the Albumin. Drains can only be done in an emergency at St. Albert or U of A. (That was an all-day exhausting experience yesterday.)

He did manage to get an excellent emergency doctor who got him into a CAT Scan.

His drain was plugged due to the mass in his abdominal area, making breathing feel tight and extremely uncomfortable. That morning he went back to St Albert at 11:30 a.m. to see a radiologist who would do a guided drain. The old one had to be removed, and another one put in because of the ascites being blocked by the mass.

It needed to be guided to make sure nothing internally gets punctured as that would add so much grief to what already is happening. Infection would be the primary concern.

He did get two litres drained, most of it from his chest cavity behind his lungs. The mass was pushing the fluid wherever it found space. The Royal Alex Hospital would be calling to remove the old and put in a new stint surgically.

His blood was low, and that was a bit of a challenge getting proper iron supplements. One of the most significant issues here is accessing a doctor in real time. Three to five day wait times are critical when someone is needing immediate attention. And emergency waits are just too exhausting.

Prayers for a healing day were requested. It was a long road ahead.

We had an appointment on Thursday with an oncologist team to discuss a possible trial. We would know more at that time how we should proceed, either by chemo protocol, trial protocol, or back to Tijuana therapies. Once all options were on the table, we would get our team to look at them and decide with Marty which course of action should be taken.

The mass in his abdominal region seemed to be the biggest issue, but once we got the CAT Scan results, we would know more. Every day was a considerable challenge. I continually prayed over Marty.

My parents' 65th Anniversary celebration was a difficult time for them as they tried to cope with what was going on. Bryan came home for a week and we made the most of a joyous occasion without Marty.

The drain tube was removed in a surgical procedure, and Marty missed his beloved grandparents' 65th Anniversary. He was in far too much pain to attend. Cancer sucks!

Teegan attended the Anniversary honoring his dad and family. He and his Uncle Bryan celebrated with lots of family and friends, making Baba and Gigi's day that much more special.

Upon arriving home, Marty spent the next three weeks finding and educating doctors on putting together a protocol that was manageable for him. Firstly, somewhere that all his supplements and IVs could be administered in a timely fashion, and all under the supervision of a doctor that would agree to the regimen. This proved to be quite the feat to accomplish.

Our medical system does not allow for these types of natural support systems and therefore some of the supplements were administered at all risk to Marty. He had to sign off any ill effects. By the time he was able to get this done his ascites had returned and was difficult to bring under control. His feet especially swelled and ached, making it very uncomfortable to get around.

On July 13, 2018, the Cross Cancer Institute in Edmonton called to say they might have a possible trial drug. Still waiting patiently for the biopsy that was supposedly sent away in March that had not yet arrived in Houston, caused concern. I pressed harder, asking for a receipt or some sort of validation of the parcel being sent. It was at this time that we were told it was never shipped and that the biopsy was too small.

Three months had passed, where we should've seen results come back. Instead, we asked for another oncologist, one more open to all of our functional science support and with the new oncologist on board she did request a second biopsy that was finally scheduled for September 20, 2018. Six months later than it was requested the biopsy was finally sent away to a lab in Houston, Texas.

In the meantime on July 25, 2018, Marty started a trial study, which included a drug called Erlotinib. It was not the ideal trial for Marty, but the other option had no spaces available for him, so he decided to take a chance on it. Going back to Tijuana was too difficult because of the ascites condition.

The trial study was to test a drug (theophylline) that has been approved by Health Canada and is naturally found in cocoa beans and trace amounts in brewed tea, but of course, these amounts are significantly less than found in therapeutic doses. Its chemical properties have demonstrated that it might be useful when combined with the type of medication called tyrosine kinase inhibitors (TKI) such as erlotinib, they can inhibit the growth factor that is sometimes altered in lung cancer. The study was to learn how effective theophylline, when administered with erlotinib, is at reducing diarrhea in patients who have metastasized advanced cancer. They would also evaluate tumour response in subjects. This trial study meant that the safety and effectiveness good or bad of the theophylline with erlotinib has on the participant, and to find out the highest dosages that can be given safely without causing severe side effects.

So it started, Marty would take one pill a day of erlotinib for the duration of a twenty-eight-day cycle. August was somewhat enjoyable, some days Marty made breakfast, and that prompted a call from his son Teegan to say his dad was doing much better. Marty continued exercising on the treadmill in spite of his swollen feet. But mid-August his ascites started up in his left lung. He then started taking small dosages of morphine to help with pain management.

Depending on the monitored results, Marty would continue for another twenty-eight-day cycle and so on until it either worked or did not work. The side effects were definitely very nasty. Skin rashes, decreased appetite, fatigue, shortness of breath, very, very dry skin, abdominal pain, vision problems, edema (swelling of the feet), and overall immune deficiency were many of the side effects. It seemed promising at first, with September's CAT Scan showing no tumour growth and actually some shrinkage from 3 mm to half a centimetre, but disappointing to the oncologist as she had hoped for some bigger changes. She decided to let him continue into month three, but by the end of October, it was clear the trial was not at all conducive to Marty's cancer.

Knight's Cabin Wellness, September 6, 2018
Robby Williams, Dr. Lisa Belanger, Corey Deacon, Marty and me.

Marty was president of Knights Cabin and dedicated his last two years to this incredible organization that allowed cancer patients and their caregivers to attend a weekend retreat on post-cancer care free of charge.

He organized a Knight's Wellness on September 6, at the Dow Centre in Fort Saskatchewan. There he spoke on the importance of living chemical free, eating organic and grass-fed, getting exercise and living with cancer by making yourself an outlier. He was powerful, his message stung the very soul of those who attended. "Never give up hope" he said, "and never let anyone steal your hope away."

Marty made an impact every time he spoke. His wellness speech at the 2017 Bryan Mudryk Golf Classic was powerful.

One bittersweet moment I will always treasure was in September. Bryan came out to visit his brother. He brought two envelopes, one for Marty and his family and one for me and my husband, Larry. Inside was an invitation to the Montréal Canadiens hockey game of our choice. It was signed by the new TSN play-by-play announcer. It took a moment to grasp that realized dream for Bryan and we all hugged and cried at the best news ever! I will always cherish the memory of both boys embracing with tears in their eyes and rejoicing at Bryan's realized life dream. Marty was ecstatic for his brother but saddened that he may not be well enough to attend a game. The days became increasingly difficult to attend the boys' hockey, get to doctors' appointments and therapies.

On November 7, Marty was admitted to the Fort Saskatchewan Hospital. Those days tested our faith, and we prayed every day for a miracle. The Bible is full of miracles, we just needed one for Marty, so he could enjoy his precious boys, his sweet family a little longer.

We were grateful for peaceful nights and painless days, although neither happened very often.

Marty's last weeks were of conversations with his boys, Teegan and Jesse, encouraging them to keep on keeping on and several days before his passing he told them they had a job to do. "Do well at hockey and do well at school," he said, and he told them, "I love you." In spite of his pain and discomfort, he managed to leave the hospital on several occasions to watch his boys play hockey at the local arena. He loved the sport so much and lived vicariously through them.

His go-to pain drugs were Maxaran, Decadron and dilaudid. The battle was beyond what anyone should have to endure.

Two weeks before passing, the lab results from Houston, Texas came in a 21-page document on what protocol might have saved Marty or at least given him more time. It came six months too late; our system failed him. I have shared his document with others in the hope it could help them. Cancer sucks!

I also sent it to his oncologist, but the hospital would not entertain protocols, not in their pre-approved medical treatments. For Marty, we will never know if it would've made a difference.

Spending many nights and some days at the hospital with Marty gave us time to discuss topics of interest, we shopped online for Christmas, and I pushed his wheelchair many miles down the hallways of the hospital, pausing occasionally to take in the sun and the snow outside the hospital windows. One evening he said, "Mom, I don't have much time."

Nothing ever prepares you for your son's death, and right to the last moment you never expect it will happen. You always pray for a miracle, that might somehow make him whole again. He said he would be home for Christmas and he was. Not how we had hoped but Marty chose his path and God embraced him throughout, carrying him many a day and night. He died peacefully on November 28, 2018. A hero he will always be.

And I will always treasure Marty's last words to me, "I love you, mom."

As I write Marty's journal the tears flow and blur my vision, I still struggle with the why and I pray that God helps us all move beyond the pain, the loss, and the heartache.

"Upward and onward. Keep on keeping on."

Chapter 16:

From My Heart To Yours

Life throws us curves balls; it strikes out and hits home runs. Many times I get asked how do I go on, how do I get through each day with so many challenging adversities? How do I remain strong and continue moving forward in spite of a marriage that did not end well, and three miscarriages between my two sons? My younger son battled for his life in a three-year cancer journey, I lost a granddaughter at her birth in 2012, then lost her dad, my first born, to cancer after his 19-month battle with cancer in 2018, and now look after aging parents and a husband who's diagnosed with Parkinson's?

Sometimes life is not fair, and those times really make you dig deep in your soul and expose who you are physically, mentally, and spiritually. It reveals your very purpose on this earth. When tragedy or life-threatening events happen to you, you start to explore that purpose, your passion, your vision, but most importantly, it's finding your reason.

Is it easy? Absolutely not! Every single day pushes you to move forward, to make choices that would determine whether you have a productive day, or choose the latter, get out of bed, or not.

The reality of death brings you to appreciate life, to find the good in the unfortunate situation, and to enjoy the smell of roses when you just sat on a thorn. The gruesome road of chronic illness makes you sympathetic to those suffering around you, to those whose fate is similar to your own journey, to those who look for hope when hope is stolen from them. Your day becomes more purposeful. When you reach out and touch their souls, helping someone in need lessens your own pain and loss and makes your road lighter, brighter, and worth living.

Firsts are difficult, I will not lie. The first Christmas was only one month after his death. We made it memorable with my dad building a Zamboni in Marty's memory for his beloved North Skeleton Lake hockey rink. That Zamboni and my dad's story went viral and put a smile on all our faces knowing Marty would have celebrated his crazy engineering tactics.

Bryan with Gigi who built a Zamboni in Marty's memory. News of this, including some videos of it, went viral on social media and across Canadian radio & television networks. (Christmas 2018)

Marty's birthday, which fell on Easter Sunday 2019, was bittersweet but also comforting knowing that he was in a good place. We embraced the heartwarming family time.

Mother's Day and my May birthday were equally difficult as it was the six-month mark. I flew to Toronto to spend it with Bryan. Last year Marty took me to a Padres game in San Diego while he was in treatment in Tijuana. This year Bryan took me to Blue Jays vs. Padres. We went to Summit Golf Course, we shopped for plants, together we celebrated with Marty.

Yes, there were tears, but also smiles and laughter too. That's the balance in life. The human nature of physical touch and feel on some days becomes an unbearable loss. You miss the text messages, the calls, and the visits, but you surround yourself with the beautiful memories and know he is smiling down on us all. Life without Marty seems surreal, but we get signs that he is with us in spirit and like his personality that can put a smile on our face, is knowing that he is always watching and close by.

Some days I tend to beat myself up. I reflect on the many modalities that Marty entertained. I saw so many flaws in our broken medical system, which leaves me with so many unanswered questions. Could I have pushed harder for better and quicker options that went beyond the standard protocol? Could we as a whole country be more accepting of western medicine working alongside functional science medicine in one big playing field where everyone's game plan is to make sure the patient scores a home run? That is my vision, to see these two conglomerates come together for the good of health and wellness conducive to each patient's need and situation versus one protocol that fits the establishment's budget. It's all about the money. I do not believe free Medicare gives us our best options. It just cannot afford to.

When the tears come, I can only remind myself to be kinder to myself and accept that I am exactly where God wants me to be. Divine strength comes in the daily blessings around me, and I am grateful for the family and friends who surround Bryan, Marty's family, and me. That support system is beyond comforting, and that is the light in a dark moment. Enjoy your moments, your loved ones, say what is needed, savor your relationships, do your happy dance and sing loudly, for life is short.

Grief is its own journey, memories become as precious as the stars in the sky, and the birds chirping in the early morning sunrise. Every day is different, but each day is a powerful message of life and love. I am blessed to have had both of my boys compellingly impact this world, each leading his own legacy that has changed lives. Every day I hold onto those positive changes and go forward into a new day knowing there might be tears, or there might be laughter, or there might be unexpected disappointments, or there might be amazing surprises, but most importantly I know going forward I Can-Cer-Vive. The road is mapped, my journey is planned, and I am where I'm supposed to be. For that, I am genuinely grateful.

xo
Terry

Author's Notes

Travis Christofferson MS writes in his book *Tripping Over The Truth*, that few words are as emotionally charged as the word cancer. It brings fear to the fearless, sadness where joy once lived, suffering, and pain so terrifying that it leaves an entire family in profound helplessness. He says, "It's a cruel killer and masterful escape artist. Those who battle valiantly, win, or lose are my heroes and hold my heart forever."

We desperately need to change our food chain, the chemical additives to our personal spaces, toiletries, green spaces, and protect our water sources from them. Globally over $100 Billion has been spent in taxpayer-funded research grants, besides the billions in donations and sponsorships that have yielded no substantial changes in survival rates. In five years it's expected one out of two will get cancer, one out of four will die. In our family, that is not a statistic, that was and is our reality.

Tripping Over The Truth is an excellent read and alongside with *Radical Remission* were Marty's two favorite books for profound cancer and post-cancer management. Dr. Barry Marshall was labeled a quack by the medical community for his claim of an unknown species of bacteria causing ulcers, he grew them, and in the act of desperation, he drank them to prove his claim. That bacteria were Helicobacter Pylori—the same bacteria that was one of the culprits of Marty's cancer cause, and I talk about that more in a later chapter. Once ridiculed, eventually, Dr. Marshall was awarded a Nobel prize for his find.

Leaky gut and gut disruption all need to be looked at more closely. Research never concludes but only continues. Warburg's War was also awarded a Nobel Peace Prize in 1931 for his work in discovering the cause of cancer. His theory postulates that, "The driver of tumorigenesis is insufficient cellular respiration (lack of oxygen) caused by an insult to the mitochondria and that damage results in the start of a cancer invasion. No disease, including cancer, can exist in an alkaline environment." He also said all healthy cells have an absolute requirement for oxygen, but cancer cells can live without oxygen - a rule without exception. "Deprive a cell 35% of its oxygen for 48 hours, and it may become cancerous." Dr. Warburg made it clear that the root cause of cancer is oxygen deficiency, which creates an acidic state in the human body.

Dr. David Angus, a leading cancer specialist who treated Steve Jobs, told CNBC's *Squawk Box*, "We must focus on prevention. Sitting is the new smoking," he said. "Go for short walks often because the health benefits are real."

Arming people with knowledge to make better and different lifestyle choices will maximize long-term health benefits. I hope this book does just that for you and your family. New research shows every year you delay retirement, you reduce the incidence of Alzheimer's by 3%. All the chapters in this book talk about our journey, all the modalities we tried, during the battle and post-cancer with both boys. Many of our family members and friends are being proactive by incorporating some of these tools to better wellness.

I teach preventative health classes weekly across Canada, so that lives can be changed, and that cancer or chronic disease is not in your vocabulary. I pray this book reaches those who need positive change, that it inspires you to know better and to do better. I pray that it gives you hope so that you too Can-Cer-Vive.

Marty, Jesse and Teegan on North Skeleton Lake. Greetings from Hockey Night in Mudrykville!

Concluding Remarks

Cancer is not a death sentence. My family can attest to that. Although we are still on the battlefield, it is reassuring and encouraging to know there are so many modalities that Functional Science has to offer that were not available even 10 years ago. Much research has been done on supplements, essential oils, therapies and nutrition; all translating into a working protocol to fight cancer when chemotherapy and radiation is not an option. It's very challenging emotionally because although much research is done, it has not been clinically tested on humans, mostly because there is not much profit in supplements, diet and oils. There are however, thousands of testimonies online that boast of their cancer-free lives because of these lifestyle changes. We are seeing positive results in our family and in everyday people who were given no hope.

As I write this book, my wish is to give hope where hope was stolen from you, to give you contact information for Functional Health Professionals, vital step-by-step therapies and chemical-free options and lifestyle changes that can help you feel better regardless of what chronic disease you or your loved one is facing today. The protocol is not easy, nor does it feel secure at times, but knowing others are paving the way by using functional science therapies and succeeding in their battle is promising and hopeful. The most precious commodity you can give yourself is to carry on your normal daily activities and enjoy each day with your family. Life is precious. Cancer sucks!

Getting the call your children have cancer is the most heart breaking, gut wrenching moment that haunts you forever. Life is never the same. It changes you and those around you forever. I got that phone call more than once, more than twice - I know well the call that comes with a diagnosis, which is why I felt it was important to share what we researched and studied when our hope was shattered. What we are doing as laid out in this book *is working*, and we will be another one of those positive testimonies.

Every cancer is different, although the causes can be similar, and every protocol can vary accordingly. Our family had to clean up toxicants, infections of the body, harmful bacteria overgrowth, and moulds; the key reasons for our battles. Testing can be done to find the causes and all significant issues stemming from them. So much has been researched in the last five years with growing successes and I am so happy to have those options for my family and many who have since contacted me.

We are all so blessed to have so many great people in Functional Health Science that are practicing prevention and supporting our survivors with making healthier choices that can nurture, heal, and help protect body cells. Always question, always research, listen to your body and make wise choices for you.

If you would like more information on prevention, or help getting a chemical-free home, or more information on essential oils, or just help in getting started for a healthier lifestyle, please contact me. My information is in the Resources page.

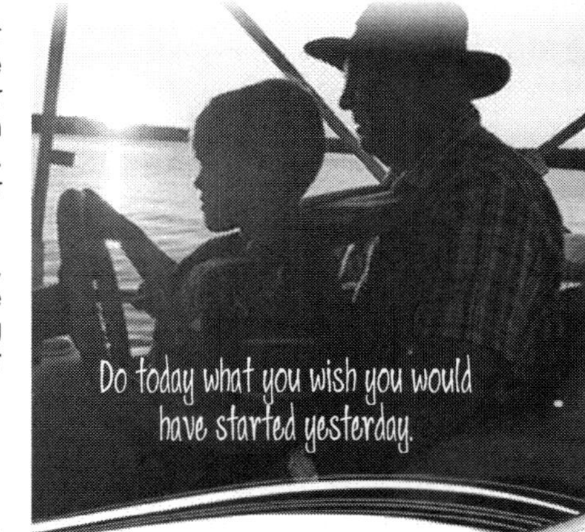

Advertisements

Check our website for a class near you, dates and times are posted: **www.oilersforlife.ca**

The Ole Fashioned Station Wellness Centre carries many holistic products like Salt Lamps Himalayan salt lamps purify the air through the power of hygroscopy, meaning they attract water molecules from the air. They also take positive ions, and when heated, the salt releases the cleansed water vapour back into the air as it expels negative ions providing better air quality in your home.

We carry a wide assortment of wellness products that are chemical-free such as laundry soap, hand and body products, makeup, toothpaste plus so much more.

Our Essential Oils selection is of top quality, and we carry a huge variety of single oils and blends, essential oil jewellery, diffusers and a good range of water features. Check our Facebook group at https://www.facebook.com/groups/837425043043638/ for weekly updates.

Health therapies are available, with a walk-in Chiropractor coming every Friday. (no appointment is necessary)

Osteopathic Manual Therapies, Raindrop Therapies, Massage Access Bars Therapy, Reiki and Reflexology, are available by trained and certified practitioners and therapists.

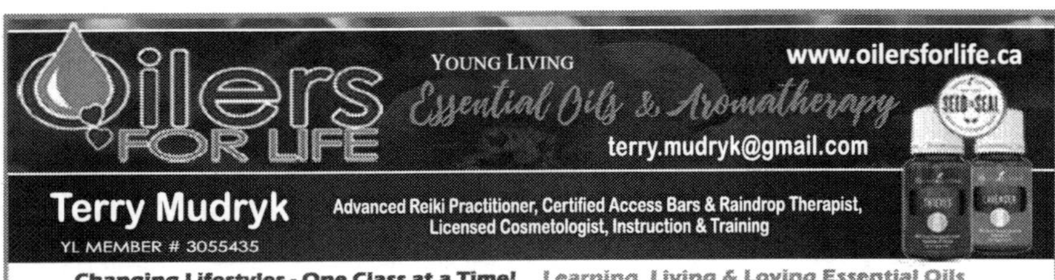

Corey Deacon, MSc, DNM, BCN. BCAMP, BCHHP, CFMP, Certified Functional Medicine Practitioner, Neuroscientist, Board-Certified Doctorate of Natural Medicine, Board-Certified in Neurofeedback, Board-Certified Alternative Medicine Practitioner, Fellow of Anti-Aging Regenerative and Functional Medicine, American Board of Anti-Aging Medicine Health Practitioner

NEURVANA HEALTH

Neurvana Health
208/209, 5589 - 47 Street, Red Deer (587-997-4649)
220A, 4039 Brentwood Rd NW, Calgary   (587-997-4649)

Resources

Terry Carolyn Mudryk, Advanced Reiki Practitioner, Certified Access Ears & Raindrop Therapist, Licensed Cosmetologist
'Ole' Fashioned Station Wellness Centre
5100 - 3rd Street, Box 369 Boyle Alberta T0A 0M0   (780-689-6736)   www.oilersforlife.ca

Corey Deacon, MSc, DNM, BCN. BCAMP, BCHHP, CFMP, Certified Functional Medicine Practitioner, Neuroscientist, Board-Certified Doctorate of Natural Medicine, Board-Certified in Neurofeedback, Board-Certified Alternative Medicine Practitioner, Fellow of Anti-Aging Regenerative and Functional Medicine, American Board of Anti-Aging Medicine Health Practitioner
Neurvana Health
208/209, 5589 - 47 Street, Red Deer, Alberta   T4N 1S1   (587-997-4649)
220A, 4039 Brentwood Rd NW, Calgary, Alberta T2L 1L1   (587-997-4649)

Axe, Dr. Josh, "Eat Dirt"

Balch, James and Phyllis, "Prescription for Nutritional Healing"

Dr. Leonard Coldwell

www.thetruthaboutcancer.com
https://www.cancer.org or www.health-science.com
www.ncbi.nlm.nih.gov/pubmed
https://www.organicfacts.net/home-remedies/15-ways-to-reduce-your-risk-of-cancer.html
https://www.organicfacts.net/home-remedies/10-best-foods-for-healthy-skin.html
http://en.cnki.com.cn/article_en/CJFDTOTAL-LCHG200601003.HTM
New England Journal of Medicine Neumann.org 345:784-789
www.healthline.com
http://www.ncbi.nlm.nih.gov/pubmed/17039854
www.scientificamerican.com
www.drwhitaker.com
http://nei.nih.gov/health/healthyeyes
http://www.health.harvard.edu/blog/vitamin-b12-deficiency-can-be-sneaky-harmful-20301105780
https://www.webmd.com -diet -slideshow
http://www.webmd.com/vitamins-and-supplements/lifestyle-guide-calcium
https://www.unilab.com.ph-articles
www.organicfacts.net
www.Dr.Mercolacancerliving.ca
https://www.sciencealert.com
www.muddyphilanthropy.ca
www.cancerresearchuk.org
http://www.ncpi.nlm.nih.gov/pubmed/25872879.5
https://drake.com/homeopthy
https://www.urmc.rochester.edu

Reflections...
"Feed your Soul"
Writing your
thoughts and visions
are very therapeutic.
Reflect and grow
in your
healing journey.
xox
Terry

Notes...

Notes...

Calm, Inspired, Courageous, Hope, Love, Strong, Motivated, Grateful, Blessed, Peace,
Terry & hubby Larry
Raising monies for the Cross
Mom (85) & Dad (89) celebrate 67 Years July 2020
Marty, Kristen, Jesse & Teegan
Sometimes self-care is exercise and eating right. Sometimes it is sitting on a sandy beach and watching a sunset. Sometimes it is thinking happy thoughts. Sometimes it is spending time with God.
KEEP ON KEEPING ON
ALWAYS REMEMBERED FOREVER IN OUR HEARTS 19/4-2018
Dad
(Squamous Cell Carcinoma survivor)
Rejoice in hope, be patient in affliction, be constant in prayer.
- Romans 12:12
The battle is real: Bryan
(2-time Hodgkins Lymphoma survivor)
Sisters Terry, Kate & Rose
(Rose is a survivor of Adenocarcinoma of the Endometrium)
My fun family

Manufactured by Amazon.ca
Bolton, ON